# U.S.-Canadian Energy Trade

# Other Titles in This Series

# Westview Special Studies in Natural Resources and Energy Management

## U.S.-Canadian Energy Trade: A Study of Changing Relationships
### Helmut J. Frank and John J. Schanz, Jr.

The United States and Canada had a close energy trade relationship for well over two decades after World War II. Petroleum products, natural gas, electricity, and coal were freely exchanged and Canada's potential reserves were believed capable of making a sizable contribution to the solution of the U.S. energy problem. On both sides of the border, there were advocates of expanded energy trade and some support for a fully coordinated North American energy policy.

But efforts to negotiate a common energy program in the early 1970s came to naught. Instead, both countries embarked on separate national programs and reduced reliance on each other's natural, technical, and financial resources. This study looks at the reasons for the failure to achieve greater harmony in the two countries' energy policies by examining contributing economic, political, ecological, resource, and other factors. The authors discuss current energy perspectives, review recent examples of collaboration on specific energy questions, and suggest lessons learned by both countries that may indicate a mutual willingness to assume more realistic positions on common energy policy issues in the future.

Helmut J. Frank is professor of economics and director of the Division of Economic and Business Research, University of Arizona. John J. Schanz, Jr., is research fellow and assistant director, the Center for Energy Policy Research, Resources for the Future.

# U.S.-Canadian Energy Trade:
# A Study of Changing Relationships

Helmut J. Frank and John J. Schanz, Jr.

Westview Press / Boulder, Colorado

*Westview Special Studies in*
*Natural Resources and Energy Management*

Published in 1978 in the United States of America by
    Westview Press, Inc.
    5500 Central Avenue
    Boulder, Colorado 80301
    Frederick A. Praeger, Publisher

Library of Congress Cataloging in Publication Data
Frank, Helmut Jack, 1922-
    U.S.–Canadian energy trade.
    (Westview special studies in natural resources and energy management)
    1. Energy policy–United States. 2. Energy policy–Canada. 3. Petroleum industry and trade–United States. 4. Petroleum industry and trade–Canada. 5. United States–Relations (General) with Canada. 6. Canada–Relations (General) with the United States. I. Schanz, John Jacob, 1923- joint author. II. Title.
HD9502.U52F73              333.7                 78-66698
ISBN 0-89158-250-9

Printed and bound in the United States of America

# Contents

## List of Figures

# Acknowledgements

This study had its origin in a conference on U.S.-Canadian energy trade relationships held at the University of British Columbia in October 1972. The participants included government, industry, and academic representatives from both countries. The conference was supported by Resources for the Future (RFF), which had also provided funding for the preparation of advance papers at the University of Arizona, the University of Denver, and the University of British Columbia. RFF subsequently sponsored the preparation of this study, which reviews and analyzes recent changes in the two countries' energy relationships through early 1978.

The authors are indebted to the conference participants for generating many of the ideas sifted in the process of de-developing this study. Particular thanks go to Professors Paul Bradley, Milton Moore and Anthony Scott of the University of British Columbia, who prepared the original background paper stressing the Canadian perspective. Thanks also are due to Bob Behr and Barbara Scott, both students at the University of Arizona, who provided valuable research assistance. Numerous colleagues gave generously of their time and advice during various stages of the manuscript preparation. Any errors of fact or interpretation, of course, are solely the responsibility of the authors.

# 1
# Introduction

The United States and Canada, two countries with strong geographical, cultural and economic ties and a long history of peaceful, neighborly relations, had a close relationship in energy trade for well over two decades after the Second World War. Canadian crude oil supplied U.S. refineries on the West Coast, in the upper Middle West and the Great Lakes regions; Canadian gas heated American homes and supplied businesses in the same areas; Canadian and American electricity crossed the borders freely; American petroleum products supplied Canadian markets for many years; and American coal fed steel mills and power plants in Ontario. These trade relationships rested on normal commercial ties, though strongly influenced by governmental policies on the provincial (or state) and federal levels in both countries. Canada's energy exports (and imports) were large, relative to the size of its energy industries. In U.S. terms, their importance was chiefly regional, though Canada was the largest foreign supplier of crude oil for a number of years, the dominant supplier of imported natural gas, and the largest foreign customer of American coal.

Until the early 1970s, Canada's potential reserves of crude oil, tar sands and natural gas were believed to be so large that their development could make a sizable contribution to the solution of the U.S. energy problem. On both sides of the border, there were advocates of efforts to establish a more permanent basis for the energy trade between the two countries and, as an essential prerequisite, for working out common policies designed to support such long-term arrangements. A coordinated North American policy was believed to hold promise of great benefits for both countries in the form of enlarged supplies of economical energy, a high degree of supply assurance and thus greater national security, and accelerated development of Canada's vast northern regions.

Efforts made in the early 1970s toward negotiating the terms of a common energy policy for the two countries came to naught. Instead, both countries embarked on separate national policies aimed at respective energy independence, with minimal reliance on each other's natural, technical and financial resources. Energy trade between them was substantially cut back; important portions of it were phased out nearly completely.

This study endeavors to determine the reasons for the failure of the two countries to achieve greater harmony between their energy policies. In the process, it examines economic, political, ecological, resource and other factors which may have contributed to the change of direction. It goes on to discuss the current energy perspectives and policy adaptations of the two countries; reviews examples of recent collaboration on specific energy questions of limited scope; and suggests some lessons learned on both sides of the border which hold promise of a more mature and realistic stance on energy policy issues in the future.

# Oil and Gas Resources and Trade

## Early Perceptions

By the end of the 1960s the energy position of the United States had deteriorated to the point where policy makers were faced with critical decisions regarding the country's long-term energy posture. Proved reserves of the two dominant energy sources, petroleum and natural gas, had been declining persistently since 1967, with the important exception of the Prudhoe Bay field on the Alaskan North Slope.[1] True, the predominant opinion among geologists[2] was that the potential oil and gas resources of the lower 48 states were still large. But even the optimists conceded that the chances of finding really giant, and therefore low cost, fields in easily accessible locations were becoming more remote.

Keeping pace with rapidly rising demand thus required either greatly increased drilling efforts in many locations onshore or an accelerating shift to regions where technical conditions were very difficult, especially in more remote locations in deep water offshore. Additionally, while the United States was richly endowed with potentially supplementary sources of liquid and gaseous hydrocarbons in the form of oil shales and coal, the technology for converting these into oil and gas had not reached the point where they constituted an economical supply source.

As the 1960s ended, the options open to the United States appeared to be between a greatly increased reliance on foreign, chiefly overseas, sources of oil or of enacting tighter import restrictions to foster development of domestic energy sources of all sorts. Under then prevailing conditions, with the international oil companies still very much in the driver's seat and oil readily available on world markets at low prices, the policy choices seemed to be quite clear, although by no means wholly pleasant: (a) relying on an energy supply which was very cheap, even by then prevailing notions but, because the role of the Middle East was bound to grow rapidly, potentially quite insecure; or (b) shifting to domestic sources which offered maximum supply assurance but would be much more costly, such as coal and shale oil. This choice was one with which the Cabinet Task Force on Oil Imports wrestled in 1969, with indecisive results; a majority, led by the chairman, Labor Secretary George P. Shultz, opted for freer trade[3] while a strong minority, including the Secretaries of Interior and Commerce, favored tighter import quotas. The President did not act on either recommendation but let events run their course.

Expansion of energy trade with Canada seemed to offer an attractive "third option" to this dilemma, which could broaden the economical oil and gas resource base available to the United States but under conditions posing a minimal risk of supply interruption for military or strategic-political reasons.

Estimates of Canadian resources had been greatly raised since discoveries in the Arctic. The Canadian Petroleum Association was estimating total potential oil reserves at 120.8 billion barrels and gas reserves at 725 trillion cubic feet (TCF).[4] In 1972 the Canadian Geological Survey, reflecting recent drilling results, further increased these estimates by 11 and 25%, respectively. Deducting volumes produced, remaining recoverable oil reserves were estimated at 128.5 billion barrels and gas reserves at 890.7 TCF (see Table 1). The gas potential was equivalent to three-fifths that of the United States, and Canada's oil potential approached 80% of the U.S. figure. Thus, if the United States were to gain access to these future Canadian supplies, the total volumes of oil and gas resources on which it could draw would be increased appreciably beyond those available within its own borders. This did not in-

**Table 1. U.S. and Canadian Oil and Gas Potential,\* as of 1972**

|  | *Oil* *(bill. bbls.)* | *Gas* *(tril. cu.ft.)* |
|---|---|---|
| Canada | | |
| Ultimate recoverable[a] | | |
| Western Canada | 28.6 | 207.4 |
| Beaufort Mackenzie | 14.7 | 117.2 |
| Arctic Island-Coastal Plain | 49.3 | 327.4 |
| Eastern offshore | 38.5 | 229.6 |
| Others | 3.3 | 19.5 |
| Totals | 134.4 | 906.2 |
| Less volumes produced[b] | 5.9 | 15.5 |
| Remaining recoverable[c] | 128.5 | 890.7 |
| | | |
| United States | | |
| Ultimate discoverable amount in-place[d] | 810.4 | 1,857 |
| Total recoverable | 258.5 | 1,857[d] |
| Less volumes produced[b] | 96.6 | 410 |
| Remaining recoverable[c] | 161.9 | 1,447 |

\*Conventional crude oil and natural gas only. Excludes natural gas liquids, tar sands, and heavy oils.
[a] Geological Survey of Canada, 1972 evaluation.
[b] Canadian Petroleum Association. Cumulative production through 1971.
[c] Includes proved reserves.
[d] National Petroleum Council, *U.S. Energy Outlook,* December 1972, pp. 72, 91.
*Source:* Appendix A.

clude Canada's Athabasca oil sands and heavy oils which represented potential sources exceeding the total volumes of conventional forms in both countries combined.[5] In addition, Canada had within its borders large reserves of uranium, thorium, and coal, as well as several good sites for large-scale production of hydroelectricity.[6]

For oil and gas, the geographical distribution of potential resources was to become an important consideration. The great bulk of Canada's potential oil and gas was located in "frontier" regions (Mackenzie Delta-Beaufort Sea, the Arctic islands and plains of the far north, and the waters off the East Coast) where exploration is difficult and costly (see Figure A-1, Appendix A). In addition, except for the eastern offshore region, the problems and costs of moving supplies to markets, once established, were formidable indeed. Proved resources from past development were nearly all located in the Prairie provinces, chiefly Alberta, but indications were beginning to multiply that their future expansion would be quite limited.[7] The realization of Canada's oil and gas potential thus depended heavily on firming up the promises of the frontier regions, and on overcoming the great obstacles to their development.

## Actual Oil and Gas Flows[8]

Geography, economics and policy decisions have shaped the marketing of Canadian oil and gas. Following the discovery of the first large oil field at Leduc, in 1947, pipelines were built to carry the oil outside the producing provinces, first to the east (1950) and then the west (1953). Western markets for oil, both in British Columbia and the U.S. West Coast (chiefly near Puget Sound) are served by the Trans Mountain Pipeline. Movement eastward is by the Interprovincial Pipeline system. This ran at first only to Superior, Wisconsin, later was extended to Sarnia, north of Detroit, and still later to the Toronto area (see Figure C-6, Appendix C).[9] In order to permit the (then) higher cost refined products made from Canadian crude to find a market, the Canadian government, in 1961, established a line of demarcation along the Ottawa Valley, which divided the markets for domestic and imported petroleum. Markets east of this line (Quebec and the Maritime provinces) were served exclusively by foreign oil, chiefly imported crude processed in Canadian refineries; markets to the west have been reserved for Canadian crude and refined products.

Canadian crude moving to Ontario destinations traverses long stretches of U.S. territory, entering at the Manitoba-

Minnesota border and continuing through Wisconsin and Michigan (one leg also crosses part of Illinois) before re-entering Canada. The total distance of U.S. territory crossed by Lakehead Pipeline, the U.S. subsidiary of Interprovincial, is 1,739 miles. In addition, for many years the system has carried large volumes of Canadian crude to U.S. refineries in the "Northern Tier" (Minnesota and Wisconsin) and to the Chicago, Detroit and Buffalo areas.

By contrast, natural gas from Canadian fields has moved to eastern markets by way of an all-Canadian system, Trans Canada Pipeline, as far east as Montreal. This system also delivers gas at border points in Minnesota, Michigan and Vermont for distribution to U.S. markets. On the West Coast, substantial volumes have been exported by West Coast Transmission and Alberta Southern Gas Company; these moved gas as far south as central California. Smaller quantities enter the Rocky Mountains at the Montana border.

Until the early 1970s, production of Canadian crude oil lagged well behind productive capacity. As late as 1970, production, at about 1.3 million barrels a day (b/d), averaged only 58% of full potential (2.3 million b/d). For many years, Canadian producers were anxious to find additional markets at home or south of the border. But their efforts were frustrated by a combination of excess productive capacity in the major U.S. producing states and low-cost foreign oil available to refiners in both the U.S. and eastern Canada. Up to 1970, export demand for Canadian oil was insufficient to offset imports into eastern Canada. Two years later, however, rising domestic and especially export demand had pushed Canadian crude production to almost 80% of capacity. U.S. fields were no longer able to increase production and the booming demand by American consumers could only be met by greater imports. As a result, Canadian exports rose by 55% in two years and Canada had become a sizable net oil exporter.

Natural gas exports also grew rapidly during this period. Despite access to the Montreal market, they constituted 43% of total Canadian sales in 1972, an even greater market share than oil exports (42%). However, Canadian gas exports had reached at least a temporary ceiling, since all developed supplies were fully committed. Canadian authorities repeatedly turned down additional export applications in order to protect the future requirements of domestic customers.[10]

### Canada's Prospective Contribution

Because of growing concern in the United States over rising energy imports, Assistant Secretary of the Interior Hollis Dole in January, 1970, requested the National Petroleum Council (NPC), an advisory industry body, to undertake a broad study of U.S. energy prospects and options. In July 1971, the council published an interim report, *U.S. Energy Outlook: An Initial Appraisal,* which made projections to 1985 on the assumption that existing policies continued without change. In December, 1972, the final report presented the results of various possible changes in U.S. energy policies designed to accelerate domestic energy supply development.

The council's task groups included broad membership of specialists from the various energy industries familiar with conditions both in the United States and abroad. Estimates of Canadian oil and gas developments to 1985 therefore represented much more than mere statistical extrapolations based on secondary information. They showed that Canada in 1985 would have available a net export balance of petroleum liquids (crude oil, natural gas liquids, and syncrude from oil sands) on the order of 2 million b/d (Table 2). On the realistic assumption that at least some imports into eastern Canada would continue, total volumes available to the United States could then run to at least 2.5 million b/d.[11] The latter figure implied a tripling of the 1970 flow of Canadian oil to the United States.

The exact size of Canada's contribution to reduced U.S. reliance on offshore sources depended heavily on what policies the United States would adopt to hold down its total oil imports. If import policy did not become more restrictive (initial appraisal assumption), Canadian oil would represent only about one-sixth of total U.S. oil import requirements in 1985

**Table 2. 1985 Projections as of 1969-72 for Canadian Petroleum Liquids Supply and Demand Balance (Thousand b/d)**

|  | 1970[a] | 1972[a] | 1985 Projection[b] | 1985 Projection[c] |
|---|---|---|---|---|
| Production |  |  |  |  |
| Crude |  |  |  |  |
| W. Canada | 1,349 | 1,647 | * | 2,200 |
| Frontier | — | — | * | 1,200 |
| Syncrude from oil sands | 33 | 51 | * | 1,000 |
| Total | 1,382 | 1,698 | 3,740 | 4,400 |
| Natural gas liquids | 90 | 127 | — | 400 |
| Total | 1,472 | 1,825 | 3,740 | 4,800 |
| Imports | 759 | 919 | 1,204 | * |
| Total supply | 2,231 | 2,744 | 4,944 | * |
| Domestic demand | 1,466 | 1,584 | 2,444 | 2,750 |
| Exports | 741 | 1,147 | 2,500 | * |
| Total demand | 2,207 | 2,731 | 4,944 | * |
| Net exports (imports) | (11) | 228 | 1,296 | 2,050 |

*Not reported.

[a] Actuals from Statistics Canada, "Detailed Energy Supply and Demand in Canada," 1970 and 1972 issues.

[b] National Energy Board, *Energy Supply and Demand in Canada and Export Demand for Canadian Energy, 1966 to 1990* (1969), pp. 55, 64, Case B (includes frontier areas).

[c] National Petroleum Council, *U.S. Energy Outlook, An Initial Appraisal, 1971-1985,* Vol. II (July 1971), pp. 50, 52.

(14.8 million b/d). However, assuming improved incentives and favorable success ratios for domestic supply sources as in Case II of the final report,[12] Canadian oil would represent nearly 30% of total imports. Both these numbers, of course, are national averages and tend to obscure the far greater importance of Canadian oil in certain regions near the border.

While U.S. imports of natural gas from Canada were expected to increase little under initial appraisal assumptions (from 1.0 to 1.15 TCF in 1985), the final NPC report projected a much more optimistic trend, to 2.7 TCF (Table 3). This upward revision reflected entirely an assumed increased availability of gas from the three frontier regions, beginning in 1980;[13] production in Western Canada was shown as virtually flat after 1975.

For petroleum liquids as well, the optimistic expectations of future availability were heavily conditional on development of new supply sources; established areas were expected to level off after reaching existing capacity.[14] The study did not provide details as to the location of future supply sources. Discoveries of crude in the frontier areas were lagging too far behind gas discoveries in 1972 to permit such a judgment to be made. The report did include a contribution of 1 million b/d of syncrude from oil sands, equivalent to more than 20% of total Canadian petroleum liquids supply in 1985.

**Table 3. Projections as of 1969-72 for Canadian Natural Gas Supply and Demand in 1985 (Billion cubic feet)**

|                   | 1970[a] | 1972[a] | 1985 Projection[b] | 1985 Projection[c] |
|-------------------|---------|---------|--------------------|--------------------|
| Net production    | 1,976   | 2,475   | 5,886              | 5,900              |
| W. Canada         | 1,976   | 2,475   | 3,533              | 2,600              |
| Frontier          | —       | —       | 2,353              | 3,300              |
| Imports           | 11      | 16      | 45                 | *                  |
| Total supply      | 1,987   | 2,491   | 5,931              | *                  |
| Domestic demand   | 1,089   | 1,339   | 2,231              | 3,200              |
| Export            | 779     | 1,009   | 3,700              | 2,700              |
| Total demand      | 1,868   | 2,348   | 5,931              | 5,900              |
| Net exports       | 768     | 993     | 3,655              | *                  |

*Not reported.

[a] Actuals from Statistics Canada, "Detailed Energy Supply and Demand in Canada," 1970 and 1972 issues.

[b] National Energy Board, *Energy Supply and Demand in Canada and Export Demand for Canadian Energy, 1966 to 1990* (1969), pp. 55, 64, Case B (includes frontier areas).

[c] National Petroleum Council, *U.S. Energy Outlook*, December 1972, p. 267.

# Other Energy Sources

Any review and interpretation of energy trade relationships between the United States and Canada must take note of the lively movement of coal and electricity across the U.S.-Canadian border. Uranium may soon join these as the fifth major energy source to be exchanged between the two countries (see Figure C-8, Appendix C).

The examination of these other energy sources requires less detail than for the dominant liquid hydrocarbons. First, the contribution of coal and electricity, whatever their regional or local importance, bulks much smaller in total U.S.-Canadian energy trade than that of the fluids. Second, in contrast to oil and gas, trade in electricity and coal for the most part follows a far more normal commercial course. That is, trade in these energy forms has been mutually advantageous to both countries, with little evidence of the friction and policy disputes that have engulfed oil and gas in recent years.

**Coal**

Although estimates of Canada's coal resources involve considerable uncertainty and the bulk of deposits is not economically recoverable with present techniques, the quantities involved are sizable.[1] The importance of coal in the Canadian energy mix has declined since the discovery of major oil and gas reserves 30 years ago, and coal accounted for only 11% of total energy consumption in 1975, compared with more than one-half in 1950. But, as in the United States, coal has a sizable market as fuel in Canadian steel mills and a rapidly expanding one as under-boiler fuel in electric power plants. Moreover, as Canadian oil and gas become insufficient to meet the country's hydrocarbon requirements, coal will become a principal source of supplementary gas and, eventually, of synthetic liquids and chemical feedstocks[2] (see Table B-3, Appendix B).

Most of Canada's coal, some 93%, is located in Saskatchewan, Alberta, and British Columbia, whereas markets are concentrated in the east, chiefly in Ontario. Until quite recently, the long distances and absence of specialized transport facilities made Canadian coal noncompetitive in Ontario with supplies imported from the United States. While production and consumption were in rough balance overall, some two-thirds of requirements were met by imports from eastern U.S. mines, while in the West similar volumes were exported, chiefly to Japan. The result has been beneficial to all parties: Canadians and Japanese obtained their coal supplies at minimum costs, while the United States gained additional employment in a chronically depressed industry as well as added export earnings.

Since the energy crisis, there have been moves toward replacing, or at least modifying, the established three-way trade pattern in coal. In particular, Ontario Hydro has been negotiating for large-scale supplies of coal from Alberta to meet its expanding thermal power plant needs.[3] This action reflects in part the sharp rise in open market prices for coal since 1973, the threatened shortages of eastern coal low enough in sulfur to meet urban air quality standards, and the development of unit trains for economic coal movement over long distances. Some American electric companies, including Commonwealth Edison Company of Chicago, have been planning the use of western U.S. coal for similar reasons.

To the extent that Ontario Hydro's moves are based on national security considerations—e.g., the fear of losing a foreign supply source during an emergency—they would parallel recent policy shifts in oil, especially the extension of the Interprovincial Pipeline to Montreal and the phasing out of exports. In the view of some respected experts, such fears may be exaggerated because U.S. exports of thermal coal to Canada represent only a small fraction of total U.S. coal production and an interruption of metallurgical coal exports would run the risk of Canadian retaliation.[4] Ontario Hydro's efforts to develop western supply sources may fall short of complete success because the Province of Alberta, which exercises policy control over its natural resources under the Canadian federal system, is strongly conservationist and environmental in outlook. Thus, it has prohibited or severely restricted strip mining of the foothill slopes, where the richest surface deposits are located, and generally appears less than anxious to approve the multiplying requests for early large-scale coal development.[5]

In summary, it would appear that for coal there is sufficient motivation for both the Canadian and U.S. governments to seek the continuation of beneficial trade so long as there are acceptable security assurances.

### Electricity

A similarly beneficial trade in energy between the two countries has developed for electricity (see Figure C-8, Appendix C). Beginning with the completion of generating facilities at Niagara Falls, in 1906, Canada has relied heavily on its abundant sources of hydroelectric power; at the end of 1975 these accounted for over two-thirds of total electric capacity, compared with only 13% for the United States.[6] These facilities are highly capital intensive and hence require a high load factor for economical operation. To attain this, systems seek to match their period of surplus capacity (slack demand) with capacity shortages (peak demand) of adjoining systems. Because population density in Canada is low and there is little diversity in the seasonal patterns between, say, Ontario and Quebec, long distance east-to-west or west-to-east movement within Canada offers little attraction, though there is substantial transmission in provincial border areas. On the other hand, demand peaks in Canada occur in winter while those in the United States, with few exceptions (northern New England and the Pacific Northwest) fall in summer. Thus there is a sizable and growing transmission from, say, Quebec to New York and Ontario to Chicago in summer and a reverse flow in winter. In addition, utilities have been assisting each other during power failures or shortages on both sides of the border in recent years,[7] with the trade balance running clearly in Canada's favor.[8] U.S. electric utilities and their customers have benefited from this trade because they saved on expensive peak load generation, while Canadian electrical agencies[9] achieved a more economical operation of their capital intensive base load plants.

The Columbia River Project, which represents the only coordinated energy project between the United States and Canada to date, has given rise to disparate evaluations. Some Canadian observers consider the treaty, which was signed in 1961, an "unmitigated disaster" for Canada.[10] Their argument cites the treaty provision which entitles the United States to obtain all of the power generated on the U.S. side, at a price one-fifth the current price, although effective flood control and hydro development could not have been undertaken without Canadian cooperation. Other knowledgeable students vigorously deny that Canada has been disadvantaged by the project in any way, and charge that the opposition, since the time of treaty negotiation and continuing until now, has been politically inspired.[11] Whatever the merits of the criticism, the dispute has not been between Canadians and Americans but between Canadians of different ideologies. The most vocal opponents of the treaty were the Socialists in British Columbia, who formed the opposition at the time the treaty was negotiated but controlled the provincial government during 1972-1975. While their criticism has been greatly toned down recently, it is possible that the Columbia River controversy has reinforced the desire of Canadian provinces to assert their power over natural resource development against the federal authorities, thus aggravating the dispute over the division of revenues from oil and gas production.

**Uranium**

Another energy source in which there exists a potential for mutually beneficial trade between the United States and Canada is uranium, the only raw material currently used to produce nuclear electricity.[12] Canada's uranium resources are large, relative to its future requirements. A recent official estimate put recoverable resources from the principal minable deposits at 558,000 short tons at up to $40 per pound of $U_3O_8$, the current market price.[13] An additional 450,000 tons are listed as "prognosticated" resources in and adjacent to minable deposits and in geological extensions to these districts. Resources in the speculative category were not reported and may be very large, since Canada's uranium resources appraisal is quite incomplete. Although one can only guess at the total figure, it may well turn out to be of a similar order of magnitude as that of the United States.[14]

One should be careful, however, not to interpret these resource data as indicating that for uranium we have found a perfect match between a willing Canadian seller and an eager U.S. buyer. The relationships between Canada and the United States in providing nuclear supplies have followed a pattern that bears some resemblance, if not in headlines, at least in character, to that found in oil and gas. In the interval immediately following World War II the United States was anxious to make provision for future uranium needs. Canada was a logical source for purchases. However, once domestic discoveries removed the immediate necessity for seeking overseas supplies, U.S. concern shifted to the well-being of its new domestic industry and the limits of its enrichment capacity. Imports were barred by the United States from 1968 to 1974. After this interlude, the recent reappearance of the United States as a prospective purchaser of uranium finds potential foreign suppliers inclined to be restrained in their commitments. Both Canada and Australia will be very certain that exports are clearly in excess of their own long range future needs as well as acceptable on other counts.

Canada has been one of the pioneers in the development of

nuclear power. Its reactors use heavy water as coolant, as distinct from the light water reactors generally used in the United States. The Canadian (CANDU) nuclear plant, although smaller than advanced U.S. models, appears to be more economical than its U.S. counterpart.[15] Its chief advantage lies in its ability to operate on natural uranium ($U_3O_8$), instead of requiring enriched uranium, as does the light water reactor.

Because of its small population and large hydro power resources, Canada's future uranium requirements are comparatively small. Canadian utilities are required to have a 15-year supply of uranium committed to nuclear facilities. A total national supply equal to 30-year requirements of all plants currently operating and scheduled to become operative during the next 10 years is required before permission to export uranium is given. Reactor capacity in 1974, including Atomic Energy Commission plants, was only 2,500 MW; an additional 12,200 MW are projected as coming into operation between 1977 and 1986, for a total 10 years hence of 14,700 MW.[16] On the basis of 5.5 tons of uranium ore required per MW over a 30-year period, required supplies total 81,000 tons. In addition Canadian uranium producers have contractual export commitments for about 110,000 short tons.[17] This leaves almost 50% of recoverable resources uncommitted to meet future export or domestic needs, not counting amounts in the prognosticated or speculative categories.

The United States, by contrast, at the end of 1976 had in operation 60 nuclear power plants with a capacity of 41.3 MW.[18] Although the nuclear construction program has been severely cut back during the past two years,[19] uranium requirements for an assumed 30-year lifetime of plants estimated as of mid-1977 to be in operation by 1986 total not quite 800,000 tons, a figure that exceeds reserves now judged recoverable at forward costs up to $30 a pound.[20] The U.S. uranium resource base is expected to prove larger than these requirements. Further geologic investigation of deposits in the continental United States is likely to raise resource estimates. Nevertheless, concern over U.S. resource limitations has given rise to pressures for the construction of uranium reprocessing plants by the mid-1980s and for an early introduction of the breeder reactor, which would greatly increase the life of uranium deposits. Both of these initiatives, however, have raised major policy questions of safety and security and were halted by the Carter administration in April 1977.

Collaboration with Canada, making uranium materials surplus to Canadian requirements and present export commitments available to supplement domestic resources, offers large potential advantages to the United States. Among these, it would enable the United States to buy sufficient time to assess the practicability of preferable long-term alternatives to the breeder, such as other types of reactors or nuclear fusion, before an irrevocable decision in favor of its commercial development must be made.[21]

# The Evolution of Energy Policies

**Efforts at Closer Collaboration**

Expanded trade in energy materials between the United States and Canada has been a subject of intermittent interest in both nations since shortly after the Leduc discovery in 1947 (see Appendix E).[1] The major issues were not whether to trade but what restraints, if any should be imposed on the flow of energy products and whether national policies impinging on energy trade ought to be modified to achieve greater harmony. In the limiting case, if all artificial obstacles to a free flow of energy materials were removed and all policy differences reconciled, a true "North American Energy Market" would be established. But arrangements short of this ultimate condition would also foster an increased flow of energy products between the two countries.

Policies to facilitate trade expansion had received wide support on the Canadian side for some two decades after Leduc. With Canadian oil wells operating far below their potential, Canada had to decide whether markets for its western oil and gas should be sought to the east, in Ontario and possibly Quebec, or to the south, in the western and north central United States.

A case could be made for either choice: an east-west flow would foster the national interest by strengthening interprovincial ties. This would be a continuation of Canadian National Policy, first proclaimed in the 1870s, designed to foster national integration.[2] The disadvantage of an east-west flow was that eastern Canada was being supplied with lower-cost energy from overseas sources.[3] To create a market for Canadian crude in the east, import quotas or tariffs would have had to be imposed and prices to eastern consumers raised. Alternatively, Canadian producers could have lowered their wellhead prices to permit Canadian crude to be sold in competition with imported oil at Montreal.

Either option would have involved a sizable loss to the Canadian economy, but the impacts on different interest groups diverged sharply. Canadian oil producers favored extension of the pipeline system to Montreal, together with protective measures designed to maintain wellhead prices; easterners benefiting from lower cost imports naturally resisted such a change. Throughout the 1960s and early 1970s, the latter prevailed, and Quebec and the Maritime provinces continued to be supplied 100% from imports.[4] Canadian producers sought additional export markets in the U.S. Great Lakes region to which they had access because overland shipments were exempt from U.S. import quotas.[5] Although Canadian producers would have preferred access to the Montreal market to the triangular trade policy, exports to the U.S. offered quite an acceptable second-best solution for them. Certainly the international oil companies preferred to keep eastern Canada open to imports from the Caribbean and Middle East. The only clear losers were residents of eastern Ontario, who were denied access to petroleum products refined from lower cost imported crude.

As to natural gas, the additional cost of an all-Canadian line, rather than one following a shorter route through U.S. territory, has been put by one analyst at $200 million annually.[6] Still, as in the case of the oil pipeline and the oil and gas lines to the West Coast, access to U.S. markets was required for such long-distance facilities to be economical. Both oil and gas pipelines are prime examples of the principle of economies of large scale, and Canadian markets alone were too small to absorb the volumes that had to be moved to bring costs down to competitive levels.

The compromise policies appeared to be widely supported

by Canadians on broad economic grounds as well. During the 1950s the country had been suffering from slow economic growth, sizable trade deficits and depressed currency values; greater exports promised to improve all of these.[7] These potential benefits were not fully realized, among other reasons because, despite formal exemption from U.S. import quotas, Canadian crude did not really have unrestricted access to American markets. Although crude imports from Canada into Districts I-IV (east of the Rocky Mountains) rose sharply between 1960 and 1969, to 341 thousand barrels a day or one-third of total crude oil imports, they were restrained by a series of technical manipulations, "jawbone" techniques and negotiations with the Canadian government;[8] in addition, imports from Canada were deducted from permissible offshore shipments to the U.S. East Coast. The purpose of these actions was to insure that increased imports from Canada would displace overseas imports and not U.S. domestic production. These measures were necessary since Canadian oil, though not as low-cost as overseas crude, was more attractive to both investors and U.S. customers than domestic crude.

U.S. proved reserves of both oil and gas increased until the mid-1960s, even though exploratory activity had declined steadily since the mid-50s. Producers in Texas and other major producing states were unable to find adequate markets for their oil and faced tough competition from Canadian crude in the Great Lakes region. There was a widespread belief that conventional domestic oil and gas supplies could continue to expand indefinitely if appropriate policies were adopted or kept (i.e., price controls were removed from gas and oil import quotas and favorable tax treatment were retained). These circumstances also explain why, during the 1960s, U.S. policy makers were unwilling to consider seriously Canadian overtures for a more permanent accommodation of Canadian energy sources in the U.S. market.[9]

By the end of the decade, however, the perspective south of the border was changing. Proved reserves of both crude oil and natural gas had begun to decline and, unless this trend was reversed quickly, production drops would soon follow.

Moreover, under the stimulus of a strong inflationary boom, U.S. demand for energy (chiefly oil and gas) was expanding at accelerated rates and surplus productive capacity was being rapidly absorbed. Energy supplies thus had to be enlarged somehow. The majority of the U.S. Cabinet Task Force had recommended a shift from import quotas to an oil tariff. This would have assured a growing outlet in the U.S. not only for Canadian oil and gas but also for Latin American production. Had this recommendation been accepted, existing U.S. import quotas would have been removed and U.S. domestic petroleum prices would have been closely linked to world market prices. A tariff of $1.35 per barrel was recommended to keep U.S. prices from falling, but stipulated imports from Canada and other Western Hemisphere sources would have been exempt from this levy.[10]

The alternative, implied by the Task Force minority in rejecting freer energy trade, was a major push toward greater U.S. self-sufficiency. Certainly the resource base for greatly enhanced output from domestic energy sources was available: inadequately explored and promising new locations of oil and gas; the country's large coal reserves; exploitation of vast shale oil deposits of the Rockies; speeding up nuclear power plant construction. Such a course would have entailed major policy shifts—higher energy prices, government support for research and development, a good deal of possible environmental damage—in a word, much greater total costs.

Closer collaboration with Canada offered the promise of a third alternative that would have meant fewer risks than removal of import quotas, on the one hand,[11] and lower costs than the autarchy route, on the other. Supporting a "Canadian option" were a century of peaceful relations with the neighbor to the north; close ethnic, cultural, economic and defense ties;[12] precedents set by farm equipment and automobile agreements;[13] and the dominant position in Canadian oil and gas operations of U.S. controlled firms.[14] In the short run, greater supplies of natural gas were unlikely to be made available to U.S. customers, unless Canada could be persuaded to modify its conservative export policy and exports of crude oil would soon approach their short-term potential. On the other hand Canada's long-run prospects for both gas and oil, based on accelerated development of the frontier regions, were believed to be excellent. A Canadian route for a pipeline to move Alaskan oil (and later gas) also held definite advantages over the all-American route, provided Canada did not delay its decisions unduly. Ecological risks appeared to be smaller,[15] markets in the American heartland could be reached more directly and probably more cheaply, and supplies from the Mackenzie Delta would become available more quickly. Small wonder that some astute analysts felt the question was not whether U.S.-Canadian collaboration was essential, but merely how it could best be realized.[16]

The major concern of U.S. policy makers was the vulnerability of eastern Canada, with its complete reliance on imported oil, to foreign events which could cause interruptions in the oil flow. They regarded it as inconsistent for the U.S. to limit its dependence on foreign oil by means of import quotas but then to draw heavily on Canadian supplies without some form of protective measures. Should overseas suppliers become unwilling or unable to satisfy the demands of eastern Canadian customers, Canada would have to consider diverting some of its U.S. exports to meet its own essential needs. No responsible sovereign government could be denied its prerogative to take such action. What was required was either a reduction in Canada's vulnerability or the provision of adequate contingency measures, or both.[17]

In Canada, most of the earlier reasons for seeking an energy arrangement with the United States still prevailed in the late 1960s. The major exception was natural gas supplies, which by then had been nearly fully committed to domestic and export markets.[18] But production of crude oil in Alberta was still far below potential and producers were anxious to expand their markets. World oil prices continued quite low, so that eastern Canadians had no reason to be any more receptive to a shift to domestic sources than they had been in the 1950s. Exports were the only option for Canadian crude and the U.S. market was the only logical export outlet.

A new factor causing concern among Canadian oil producers was the discovery of crude oil on the Alaskan North Slope. This oil could be moved to markets in the U.S. either by constructing a pipeline across Alaska, followed by tanker shipment to West Coast ports, or by an overland pipeline across Canada into the U.S. heartland. If the United States went it alone, Canadians faced the loss of their market in the Pacific Northwest, since Canadian crude might be displaced by supplies from the new source.[19] More important for the future, an all U.S. Trans-Alaskan oil pipeline would mean an indefinite delay in an outlet for Mackenzie Delta oil, and thus would retard development on the frontier. Running the Alaskan pipeline through Canada, on the other hand, would offer the most rapid as well as the least-cost manner of moving any Canadian oil south. Finally, Canadian as well as American environmentalists object to the considerable risks of spillage which tanker shipments of Alaskan oil would present for their western shore, especially in the Juan de Fuca Strait.[20]

**The Emergence of Autarchy**

Canadian desire to work out an accommodation on energy with the United States was far from unanimous by the late 1960s. Eastern Canadians would certainly still object to being deprived of low cost energy if the United States insisted on import restrictions. A group of strong nationalists, led by the Waffle faction of the New Democratic Party, opposed closer ties with the United States generally, on the ground that this would insure further dominance of U.S. interests over the Canadian economy.[21] Some intellectual leaders, among them Professor Eric Kierans, argued that increased exports of raw materials, financed by large inflows of U.S. capital, would create few jobs and would drive up the value of the Canadian dollar, and thus tend to make Canadian manufactured goods noncompetitive in export markets.[22] Finally, there was a growing group of environmentalists in Canada (and in the United States) who questioned the advisability of rapid development of the country's frontier resources, on the ground that the benefits would accrue chiefly to foreigners while the costs, in terms of ecological damage, early resource exhaustion and upset life styles, would be borne exclusively by Canadians. These dissenting groups were sometimes quite vocal, but their number in the late '60s was small, far from sufficient to sway the majority from its desire to explore the feasibility of negotiating an energy agreement with the United States.

During the next few years, however, there occurred a series of events which undermined the foundations of cooperative energy policies in North America. These culminated in the adoption by Canada, in late 1973, of a new National Energy Policy designed to make that country largely energy self-sufficient by the end of the decade. The United States, in 1974, declared a policy of "energy independence" under which Canada would receive essentially the same treatment as the overseas oil producing countries which, as members of OPEC, had quadrupled the price of oil on world markets (and some of whom had imposed an embargo on shipments to the United States during the fourth Arab-Israeli war). The idea of a coordinated North American energy policy by late 1973 was dead. In this section, the major events contributing to this policy shift, enumerated by year in Appendix E, are outlined and reasons for their occurrence are explored.

The events begin, chronologically, with the imposition in March, 1970, of mandatory controls on Canadian crude oil imports into Districts I-IV. This followed a virtual doubling of these shipments beyond the level formally agreed upon by Canada in 1967, following secret negotiations.[23] Next came two denials by Canada, in 1970 and 1971, of applications for additional exports of natural gas, on the grounds that the reserves sought were not surplus to Canada's own needs (using the established 25$A_4$ formula).[24] Also in 1971, the Canadian government acted to prevent the sale of Home Oil Company, an independent producing company, to a subsidiary of an American firm, Ashland Oil Co. There were clashes over the environmental damage that might be inflicted on Canada by large-scale movement of North Slope crude oil through the Northwest Passage (stimulated by the pioneer voyage of the

American icebreaking tanker Manhattan).[25] In August, 1971, Canadian hostility (as that of some other American trading partners, especially Japan) was aroused by the imposition of a 10% surcharge on imports into the United States, as part of President Nixon's "New Economic Policy."[26] During 1971 and 1972, permissible Canadian imports into the United States were repeatedly increased until, by early 1973, all restrictions had been virtually removed.[27] In February and March, 1973, Canada enacted export controls on crude oil and finished products and in June the first reduction in crude exports was made.

In the fall of 1973, the Province of British Columbia reduced exports of natural gas to the United States by more than 18%. Although the cause was inability to maintain production in the face of well flooding, the full impact was placed on American gas consumers.[28] The price of Canadian gas was increased sharply, effective January 1, 1974, and the border price was set at a minimum of 105% of the domestic price. When the Federal Power Commission had not acted on the new policy within one year, the National Energy Board notified the parties that exports would be terminated within three days unless the higher price was accepted.[29] In September 1973, Canada imposed price controls on domestic crude oil and refined products and place a tax on exports designed to equalize the cost of Canadian crude for U.S. customers with that of overseas crude.[30]

The outbreak of fighting in the Middle East in October, 1973, the ensuing embargo of oil exports to the United States and other nations aiding Israel, and the initiation of cumulative production cutbacks by Arab oil producers, greatly accelerated the shift of Canadian energy policy. While Canada itself was not on the Arab embargo list, by late 1973 its imports of crude oil fell short of requirements by some 100,000 b/d (about 10% of refinery demand in Quebec and the Maritimes).[31] This could have been the result of the general tightening of world oil markets. However, there were reports of Arab exports to Canada being held up because every barrel reduction of Arab oil available to that country would result in one less barrel of Canadian oil exported to the United States; because most foreign crude oil destined for Canadian refineries was landed at Portland, Maine (for shipment through the Portland-Montreal pipeline); and even because tankers headed for Canadian ports were reportedly diverted on the high seas to U.S. destinations.[32] Regardless of the basis of these reports, the Canadian Government decided to forestall potentially more serious problems by a series of countermeasures. Efforts were made to find additional supplies of heating oil from overseas sources (in view of the oncoming winter season): consumers were asked to practice voluntary fuel conservation; western Canadian crude was moved to eastern refineries by way of the Great Lakes and the St. Lawrence Seaway as long as these were open, and then through the Panama Canal;[33] and the reduction of exports to the United States was accelerated. Discussions with U.S. officials were resumed. Donald S. Macdonald, Canada's Minister for Energy, Mines and Resources, however, did not attempt to reopen the question of the Alaskan oil pipeline with John A. Love, Assistant to the President for Energy, and in early 1974 Congress enacted the law permitting construction of Alyeska, the all-U.S. facility.

At about the same time, the Canadian government moved to replace its existing national oil policy, which divided Canada into two segments separated by the Ottawa Valley Line, with a new policy designed to fit the changing realities of the world (and Canadian) energy situation.

The new policy contained seven major elements:[34]

1. Abolition of the Ottawa Valley Line and creation of a single national oil market for Canadian oil;
2. Use of escalating revenues to foster national security and self-sufficiency;
3. Establishment of a publicly owned Canadian petroleum company to expedite exploration and development;
4. Early completion of an extension of the Interprovincial Pipeline to Montreal, and to other points as required (previously announced);

5. Intensified research on oil sands technology to foster rapid development;
6. Rapid development of frontier and non-conventional resources to replace declining output in western Canada; and
7. Gradual removal of oil price controls until prices approached world levels. Gas prices to move to full commodity values.

The dream of a North American energy market had ended. Why? Did the policies and actions of the U.S. government contribute to Canada's turning away from energy trade with the United States? Or did the change reflect forces beyond the control of either country? Were the actions under the control of either country? Were the actions of officials of both governments reasonable? Did they benefit their respective countries? Were there better alternatives for either or both? These are intriguing questions on which the record sheds considerable light, though the answers are by no means definitive and equally acceptable to all students of U.S.-Canadian energy trade relations.

# The Bases of Energy Policies

There is no lack of ready explanations for the failure of U.S.-Canadian energy trade negotiations to succeed during the early 1970s, or rather for the inability even to get them off the ground. The list ranges from rising Canadian nationalism through a negative attitude on the part of U.S. officials. Finding arguments is easy; sorting out their respective merits and relative importance is not. This chapter examines the major explanations that have been advanced as a basis for forming a judgment on the events of the period. Five major topics are considered: nationalism, environmental concerns, national security, actions of negotiators, and changing perceptions of the energy positions of the two countries.

## Nationalism

Canada, in its modern history, has never been a leader among countries advocating free trade. Its manufacturing industries have received a high degree of protection since the 1870s because it was felt that they needed time to grow strong enough to withstand foreign competition but, typically, the "infants" have never quite reached adulthood.[1] In raw materials and agricultural products generally, where Canada has a comparative advantage, Canada had built up a worldwide export market. Its energy trade pattern, as we have seen,[2] was triangular with large exports of crude oil and natural gas to the United States and overseas imports of petroleum to the eastern provinces. By the early 1970s, however, a new wave of nationalism was spreading among Canadians and threatening to affect sectors heretofore governed by free trade policies. This trend manifested itself in the 1971 platform of the New Democratic Party (NDP), which pointed out that Canada was vastly inferior to the United States in population size, that it was rich in natural resources which its large neighbor to the south coveted and that these resources were controlled by foreigners interested in keeping Canadians to a status of "hewers of wood and carriers of water."[3] The party received 27% of the popular vote. A novel widely read in Canada[4] depicted a U.S. "elephant" taking possession of a Canadian "mouse's" Arctic island gas by force.

More extreme manifestations of Canadian nationalism took the form of broad anti-Americanism. Radical intellectual leaders and the media, in particular, pointed to what they saw as evidence of aggressive U.S. foreign policy, of which there were constant reminders in the form of the many Vietnam draft evaders who had taken refuge in Canada. Pressures grew to limit, as far as possible, "corrupting" cultural influences that continually cross the border.[5]

In the economic sphere, three major arguments were advanced: (1) American control over Canada's depletable resources (minerals and fossil fuels) would result in their premature exhaustion, leaving future generations of Canadians impoverished; (2) Canadians stood to benefit little from raw material exports as long as their nation's resources were controlled by foreign investors (since the dividends would flow abroad); and (3) large-scale foreign investment needed to finance northern resources and transport facilities would drive up Canadian exchange rates and make Canadian manufactures noncompetitive in export markets. Since most manufacturing was labor intensive while raw materials production was generally capital intensive and required little labor (at least after the initial construction stages), energy development would tend to increase further the high level of unemployment prevailing in Canada much of the time.[6]

Each of these arguments lends itself to objective analysis which can separate truth from fiction, and cool heads north of the border did take issue with each of the points raised. Thus, whether fossil fuel resources should be developed rapidly or slowly is a question of future price expectations (embodying technological change, consumption rates and policy options) and the social discount rate.[7] Reasonable opinion can differ on the outlook, and thus the best policy for the future.

Foreign investment helps Canada realize its comparative advantage in raw materials and thus achieve a higher level of real income;[8] the distribution of the proceeds (economic rent) can be altered by changes in taxation.[9] Finally, the exchange rate structural impact, while it rests on a valid notion, is likely to be limited in both size and duration.[10]

These counterarguments, however, were more effective in scholarly circles and among moderate political leaders than among the public at large. What shaped Canada's actions in the early 1970s was the belief, however subjective, that its national interests were being undermined by continued American economic "domination" and that the country could not be truly independent until this influence was heavily curtailed. The energy sector was critical to any effective change of course. A new national energy policy, restrictive foreign investment laws, higher taxes on raw materials, and a national oil company all were needed if Canada's national aspirations were to be achieved.

## Ecology

Concerns for the ecological impact of developing Canada's energy resources were closely tied to some of the nationalistic views. One argument stated that producing and transporting the energy resources in the Canadian North (Mackenzie Delta-Beaufort Sea and the Arctic Islands) would inevitably inflict irreversible damage to the delicate ecology, both land and water, disturb animal life, and upset the life style of the natives. As in the western region of the United States, there was serious concern over the socio-economic impact of many large developments in sparsely populated, isolated areas.

Damage from large-scale development of Athabasca tar sands, with its problems of disposing of huge volumes of residue, also would be immense. In both cases it was argued that development should only be undertaken when the resources were absolutely needed within Canada and not for the benefit of foreigners.

Environmentalists in Canada, as in the United States, also questioned the advisability of using the Northwest Passage for moving Alaskan North Slope oil to the U.S. East Coast. They argued for an extension of the three-mile national limit to 12 miles, since tankers could make the trip within the latter and entirely avoid Canadian waters. They also objected to the Alaska oil pipeline because of potential oil spillage, as pointed out earlier. Interestingly, there was no opposition to plans to construct several large export refineries in the Canadian Maritime provinces, which needed the employment and revenues badly—one more indication that environmental concerns have less leverage with the poor than with the well-to-do.[11]

The effect of ecological concerns on northern energy development in Canada was little different from that in the United States. U.S. ecology groups were parties to the delay of final approval for the Alaska oil pipeline until Congress approved its construction during the Arab embargo, in early 1974. Such groups have actively intervened in decisions involving the location of off-shore acreage for oil and gas exploration, shale oil development, and many other energy related activities.

A reasonable view of ecological concerns is that the issues should be examined carefully, that all technologically and economically feasible precautions against environmental damages should be taken by project developers, and that the development should then proceed if comprehensive benefit-cost calculations indicate a project's social merits, considering alternative options.[12] Such a policy is likely to be followed by Canadians as well as Americans where the energy resources and facilities are required to serve consumers within the nation's borders.

The issue in Canada, however, was that development was believed by many primarily to benefit the United States. Given this point of departure, any significant damage to Canada's ecology would be sufficient to throw the benefit-cost balance against the project from the Canadian perspective. Any other outcome would have had to address first the question of an equitable sharing of the benefits from Canadian resource development.

## National Security

The official position of the U.S. government was that it could not consider a permanent arrangement for Canadian oil in the U.S. market as long as eastern Canada was supplied exclusively by imported oil.[13] The reason was that Canada, in case of interruption of its imports, would have to divert some of its exports to meet the needs of its eastern consumers. It was illogical, U.S. officials argued, for the United States to impose import quotas on overseas shipments while Canada remained exposed.

Canadians viewed this condition as unreasonable. In their view, the position of the two countries differed fundamentally. The United States was exposed to the Arab "oil weapon" because of its support of Israel against the Arabs while Canada, as a smaller power following a more evenhanded policy, ran little risk of being affected by a renewed conflict. More important, Canada apparently was unable to obtain a clear assurance of an equal commitment from the American side,[14] no doubt because the United States no longer had any excess crude oil capacity after April 1972.

The Canadian view of future contingencies that could impact on Canadian oil imports was clearly too limited, as events in late 1973-74 confirmed. The flow of oil to world markets was affected not only by events stemming directly from active fighting in the Middle East but from the cutbacks in crude production made by the OPEC countries, designed to validate the price increases they had adopted. Ironically, although the U.S. view had proved to be correct, the outcome was not the removal of an obstacle to a North American energy policy but support for a Canadian nationalistic solution.

## Negotiations and Negotiators

Negotiations between the representatives of nations reflect not only the factual situation at that time but to some unmeasurable degree the style and skills of the negotiators. Press reports and public recollections of those attending various U.S.-Canadian meetings refer to "gruff rebuffs" of delegations,[15] of "unreasonable demands," and even to the President of the United States being shocked at how the Canadians "look down your throat."[16] Among U.S. "demands," made in the September, 1971 talks following the imposition of the U.S. import surtax, was one that Canada balance its merchandise trade with the United States. Canadians considered this unreasonable since Canada ran a large deficit on invisibles, primarily for interest and dividends on U.S. investments in Canada. Balancing merchandise trade would have meant continued large inflows of U.S. capital just to offset service on prior investments.[17] Also, the trade surplus was widely expected to be of short duration. Another issue raised at the same time was revision of the automobile pact, which could have created large-scale unemployment in Canada.[18] The issue which caused the largest resentment in the United States, however, was the imposition of an export tax on Canadian crude oil and petroleum products at a time when Canadian consumers continued to enjoy prices controlled at substantially lower levels.[19] This policy earned for Canadians an image of using OPEC actions to profit at U.S. expense.[20] This further hindered serious discussion of a coordinated energy policy between the two countries.

From an economic point of view, the Canadian position appears fully justified and the American official reaction ill advised. The Canadian export tax was designed to raise the delivered price of Canadian oil to equal that of the world price, and it was made in response to previous increases made by the OPEC countries, not in advance of them.[21] Canadians point out, correctly, that every barrel of oil which they exported to the United States would have to be replaced by an additional barrel imported at the world price; accepting a lower return on their exports would have entailed incurring a net loss. Secretary of the Treasury William E. Simon,[22] not coincidentally, was the first American official to admit the validity of this reasoning.[23] The failure of others to see this point confirms widespread reports of either disinterest or lack of knowledge, or both, on the part of high U.S. diplomats[24] during the early '70s. They were, of course, heavily involved in the Vietnam war and in relations with the USSR and China. Western Hemisphere, including Canadian, problems were assigned a distinctly lower priority. By 1973, moreover, the preoccupation with Watergate "began to erode all foreign policy initiatives with the exception of China," according to one inside account.[25]

Criticism should not be confined to U.S. officials, however. Canadian policy, whatever its basic logic from the viewpoint of that country's interests, appears to have been poorly executed as well, in the views of some knowledgeable observers.[26] While Prime Minister Trudeau reported that his proposals for "reciprocal undertakings" were rebuffed by U.S. officials in December, 1973, U.S. negotiators had felt equally negative about Canadian reaction to their initiatives three years earlier.[27]

## Concluding Observations

In the final analysis, unless one assumes gross incompetence on the part of officials on either side of the border (more probably on both sides), one must search for more basic explanations of the failure to arrive at a set of more complementary energy policies. One obvious key area is the changing energy position of both countries during the early 1970s.

While estimates of Canada's resource *potential*[28] made in the early '70s were impressive, the trend of *proved,* i.e., assured reserves of both oil and gas was causing increased concern. As we have seen, under existing policies, natural gas reserves in excess of Canadian needs had been fully committed by late 1970, and excess crude oil capacity had been absorbed by late 1972. There had been no new large discoveries in established areas for a number of years. Proved reserves of crude oil were declining and the trend of natural gas reserves was erratic. Drilling in the frontier regions had yielded substantial volumes of gas, but far from enough to support new pipelines. Little oil had been found in the north and results of exploration off the eastern shore were also disappointing. Prospects for rapid development of the tar sands were dimming because of rapid cost escalation and continued technical problems encountered by the one completed plant.

In the United States, crude production reached a peak in 1970 and Texas production reached capacity beginning in April, 1972. Supplies to natural gas customers were curtailed beginning in 1969. The U.S. energy supply deficit acted like a sponge to absorb Canadian oil. The interests of the two countries had reversed completely from those of the earlier period. Whereas Canada had been anxious to obtain permanent outlets for its production in the '50s and '60s, by 1972 it had no difficulty selling its U.S. customers all it could produce. The United States, which had been reluctant to accommodate Canada's desire for a permanent position for its energy in the American market while its own production was below potential, by the early 1970s had become an eager advocate of adding Canadian energy to its secure supply stream. It had little to offer to Canada in return, however.

Thus, both countries had been advocates of closer collaboration in energy trade and energy policies, but at different times; there was never a coincidence of the countries' interest in collaboration at any single time. Lack of understanding, absence of clear national policies and personality conflicts all may have contributed to the failure of contacts to blossom into serious negotiations. In the end, however, it was basic developments beyond the countries' control which pointed to separate energy paths rather than a common one.[29]

# 6
# Current Perspectives

Having reviewed the history of U.S.-Canadian energy trade relationships and the reasons why efforts at a closer integration of the two countries' energy economies came to naught, it remains to consider the present energy outlook of each. Such a discussion should include both the "objective" factors— resources, technology and economics—and the more "subjective" considerations entering into the shaping of the respective national policies. This brings us to the final range of questions: what has been learned, on both sides of the border, from the turbulent events of recent years? what possibilities remain for collaboration on specific issues rather than broad policies? what evidence is there that the two countries are beginning to pursue more realistic paths in their energy trade relationships, leading to a broad consensus both nations can accept as being in their own national interests and mutually beneficial?

## The Canadian Perception

Canadian energy policy has evolved during the past few years to a point where it now offers a general framework, if not a detailed plan for specific actions in individual areas. The primary influences shaping the policy have been the great price increases in world oil, the continuing danger of future import interruptions, negative developments concerning Canada's own energy resources and their availability, the growing feeling of nationalism and the considerable economic and political difficulties the country has recently experienced.

*37*

The broad policy guidelines under which specific energy decisions are made were spelled out by the Minister of Energy, Mines and Resources, before the House of Commons on April 27, 1976.[1] The starting point is the assumption that the country should limit its reliance on imported oil, both because the cost of large imports would be difficult to meet and because supplies may not be available in the mid-80s and beyond. Canada's overriding goal thus is "energy self-reliance," defined as reduced vulnerability to unanticipated changes on the world market. The specific target calls for reducing the country's net oil imports in 1985 to one-third of total oil demand, or about 800 thousand barrels a day (tb/d). In the absence of special policy initiatives, it was estimated that net oil imports would range between 950 tb/d and 1.2 mm b/d in 1985, or 40-47% of domestic demand. (See Appendix C for recent U.S.-Canadian energy trade data.) All other facets of the policy are directed at supporting the reduction in oil imports. They include holding down the growth in energy consumption, maintaining self-reliance in natural gas, and stimulating the development of hydrocarbons from non-traditional sources. Specific instruments for implementing the policy range from appropriate energy pricing to increased Canadian content and participation in energy projects.[2]

*Oil*

In the spring of 1974 the National Energy Board (NEB) held extensive hearings on the subject of oil exports. Based on the evidence presented, the board adopted a "protection procedure" designed to limit exports when 10 years of Canadian requirements for crude oil and equivalent feedstocks could not be assured. The board also ruled that periodic hearings should be held to determine potential oil producibility, domestic liquids requirements and surpluses available for exports. (See Appendix D for export formula.) Such hearings were held in April 1975 and October 1976 and the findings were published most recently in February 1977.[3]

On the basis of its 1974 examination of Canadian crude reserve additions and likely development of supplementary sources (synthetic crude from tar sands and heavy oils), the board concluded that Canadian liquid fuel supplies would decline continuously and steeply at least until 1985. Reversal thereafter depended on a greatly increased contribution from oil sands. Since Canadian oil demand was expected to increase, even with strong conservation measures, volumes surplus to Canada's needs would diminish rapidly. The government therefore announced, in March, 1975, that exports of light crude would continue to be reduced until they were phased out entirely by 1983. With extension of the Interprovincial Pipeline to Montreal this was moved up to 1980.[4] Only exports of heavy (Lloydminister type) crudes, for which the Canadian market is limited, could continue after that time.

The board's most recent assessment reflected a forecast of declining additions of light crude reserves from established areas in Western Canada; no additional construction of tar sands plants after completion of the syncrude project, which will begin production in 1979, until after 1985, and no contribution from any frontier area. (Appendix Tables B-1, B-2 and B-3 and Figure B-1). These assumptions appeared to be well supported by available evidence. Western Canadian proved reserves have continuously declined since 1969; no major discoveries had been made since the mid-1960s. Serious technical and economic difficulties have been encountered by both tar sands plants. The syncrude group survived only with the direct participation of the two provincial governments and the National Oil Company, PetroCanada. Additional plants are likely to depend on the development of *in-situ* methods, since the bulk of tar sands deposits are covered by thick overburdens and cannot be mined economically. Exploration in the northern frontier areas, both the Mackenzie Delta-Beaufort Sea and the Arctic Islands, has discovered very little oil and so far no commercial quantities have been found off the East Coast.

Prospects for the longer term are not altogether gloomy, however. NEB projections of supplies envisage additional plants beginning in 1987-88. Bitumin deposits in the Cold

Lake area of Eastern Alberta, are expected to become near-economical; Imperial Oil Company has applied for approval of a plant[5] and Husky Oil Ltd. and Pacific Petroleums Ltd. have proposed heavy oil upgrading plants in the Lloydminister, Saskatchewan area.[6] The possibility of finding deposits of sufficient size to make extraction economical in the frontier regions still exists, though on a scale much smaller than was earlier thought.[7] Imperial remains particularly optimistic with regard to the potential off the East Coast, though further north than the areas explored to date.

The renewed optimism is based in large measure on progress achieved in removing a series of previously existing obstacles to increased oil and gas exploration. One of these was a sharp dispute between the federal and provincial governments over allocation of extra revenues resulting from escalation in oil prices in 1973-74. The western producing provinces had raised royalties levied on oil and gas production on provincial lands. The federal government retaliated by eliminating their deduction from federal income taxes. This reduced after tax earnings of private operators, who cut back exploration sharply. Since 1975 concessions have been made by all levels of government and additional exploration incentives instituted;[8] subsidies also are being granted for syncrude production from tar sands. Second, the industry has apparently accepted the presence of PetroCanada, although objections over its preferential position for exploration on federal lands is still being heard.[9] Finally, Canadian crude prices, which were some $4 per barrel below world prices, are being rapidly adjusted upward, following agreement between producing and consuming provinces in mid-1977. The adjustment process should be completed on January 1, 1979, when the Alberta wellhead price for light crude is scheduled to go to $13.75 per barrel. These price increases reflect a broad consensus on the necessity of having Canadian oil prices closely related to world prices in order to encourage conservation and supply development.[10]

Nothing succeeds like success, and Canadian policy makers no doubt are most pleased over the fact that 1977 saw the first significant oil discovery in Western Canada in nearly a dozen years. Although precise data are still shrouded in confidentiality, successful drillings by Chevron Standard Ltd., Amoco Canada and others hold promise of a major new field in the West Pembina area of Alberta.[11] Its significance lies largely in the fact that traditional areas had been widely considered to hold little promise of yielding large new finds of oil (in contrast to gas), but that drilling in deeper strata proved this view incorrect. The consequence is a renewed exploration boom which is straining all available resources.

In sum, while Canada's oil prospects appear far from glowing, there is a fair chance of attaining the 1985 "self-reliance" target. Prospects beyond that are far from clear. The NEB projections show total liquids supplies, excluding frontier areas, leveling off in the late 1980s at about half their peak rate of the early '70s (960-1,010 tb/d).[12] Given appropriate conditions—tight world supplies and rising real prices—and some luck, output could well be larger. But all sources, except possibly the eastern offshore area, are bound to be high cost, pose major technological problems, and require long lead times. Thus, no one in a responsible position views the long term future as optimistically as many did until a few years ago.

*Gas*

In contrast to oil (at least prior to the West Pembina find), Canada's natural gas position has continued relatively favorable, and earlier fears that exports would have to be reduced in order to avoid domestic shortages have not been borne out. Reserve additions in established areas of Alberta and British Columbia have matched and at times exceeded the volumes required by the domestic market plus contractual export commitments. In addition, large deposits have been found in the Mackenzie Delta-Beaufort Sea region and the Arctic Islands. While these are not yet adequate to support expensive transmission lines to major markets,[13] the Polar Arctic group filed an application for construction of a pipeline with the NEB in late 1977. In the case of the Mackenzie Delta gas, the Gas Arctic proposal, which was rejected by Canadian authorities, would have permitted shipment of Canadian along with Alaskan gas to markets in Canada and the United States. The Northwest Pipe Line (formerly Alcan Gas), which has been approved instead, makes provision for subsequent linkage of a proposed lateral from the delta. In view of the current ample supply position in Alberta, however, there is little pressure to proceed with its construction, at least until the Northwest Pipeline is completed and pending native claims are settled.[14] There is no consensus at this time on whether the gas will in fact be needed to meet Canadian demand by 1985-1990; much will depend on just how successful exploration in established areas continues to be in the next few years, and also on the progress of the Polar Gas proposal. The June 1977 projections (Appendix Tables B-4 and B-5 and Figure B-2) still showed declining availability after 1985, forcing a phaseout of exports, but these may now be out-of-date. For the present, export volumes to the United States are being maintained and will be temporarily increased under a recently concluded "time swap" agreement.[15]

The turn around in Canada's gas prospects is of very recent origin. Only two years ago, officials had anticipated that serious gas shortages would arise by 1983 and exports would have to be phased out to meet domestic needs. In fact, western Canada has developed a gas "bubble" of uncommitted reserves which reached an estimated 7 trillion cubic feet by mid-1977[16] and which has apparently continued to grow since then. Clearly, there is a lot of gas yet to be found in the Alberta foothills and Eastern British Columbia regions. The potential of these areas has been so rapidly developed with the aid of strong incentives in the form of rapidly rising field prices, especially on exports. On the principal that gas should be sold at its full commodity value, border prices for sale to the United States were increased, in a series of steps to Can. $2.28/Mcf effective September 23, 1977 (equivalent to about U.S. $2.16).[17] Prices for domestic sales lagged behind but were to rise to $1.85 per million Btu at Toronto on February 1, 1978.[18] Not only was a consensus reached between producing and consuming provinces on the basic principle of pricing, but progress toward its implementation has been rapid. Considering the many conflicting interests which have clashed recently in Canada, this constitutes no mean achievement.

## The U.S. Perception

The events of late 1973-74, which included both sharp increases in world oil prices and the use of the "oil weapon" by Arab oil exporting countries, brought home to the United States with full force the realization of its vulnerable energy position. There is no need to consider here the arguments over the responsibility for the dramatic changes which occurred in world oil markets during the early 1970s and, in particular, whether timely action by the U.S. government could have altered the outcome of bargaining between the producing countries and the major international oil companies.[19] What is very clear is that control over oil production shifted dramatically from the companies, and therefore from normal market forces, to the exporting countries, and therefore governmental action. OPEC, which for the first 14 years of its life had been little more than a paper tiger, thus became able to transfer the bulk of the economic rent generated by the low cost producing fields, especially in the Middle East, from oil importing countries to the exporting nations. The role of the international oil companies was reduced from that of dominant decision makers and profit sharers to technical consultants and marketers.[20] Thus, the determination of world oil supplies and prices has been removed from the control of U.S. or friendly nations and shifted to that of those whose interests may not always coincide with the view from Washington or Houston.

The initial reaction of large segments of the American public was to blame the shortages and increase in energy prices on a conspiracy of the major oil companies. The remedies variously called for have included price controls, vertical and horizontal divestiture of the largest companies, and even a shifting of some responsibilities from commercial organizations to a new public corporation.[21] The executive branch responded by proclaiming a "Project Independence" designed to free the country from reliance on importation of oil over a period of years.[22] This was to be achieved by a combination of increased supplies of domestic oil and gas, a shift to coal and nuclear generated electricity, development of supplementary and new sources, and conservation in use. The original projections[23] rested on extremely flimsy foundations, including questionable assumptions of the resource base, the rate of technological progress, costs, and political constraints. Subsequent revisions[24] reflected much more thorough economic analysis. Taking into account measures passed by Congress in late 1975-1976, one scenario showed oil imports in 1985 as 7 million b/d, slightly below the 1976 level.

Among policies already enacted were increased auto efficiency standards, decontrol of crude oil prices over a period of 40 months, opening of the naval reserves, shifting of electric power plants from oil to coal where feasible, and creation of an oil stockpile. Additional Ford Administration proposals included decontrol of natural gas prices, easing of air quality regulations, revision of offshore drilling rules, and a massive research and development program for synthetic and substitute fuels. If these were enacted as well, Federal Energy Administration (FEA) estimated 1985 imports as low as 4 million b/d.

Shortly after taking office, in January 1977, the Carter Administration formulated its own energy proposals and submitted them for Congressional action.[25] The proposals list three "overriding energy objectives:" reduced dependence on foreign oil and vulnerability to supply interruptions in the short run; imports sufficiently low to "weather the period when world oil production approaches its capacity limitation" in the intermediate term; and development of renewable and inexhaustible energy sources for the long run.[26] The specific oil import target for 1985 was set at 6 million barrels/day, about one-eighth of total energy consumption and less than 40% of the level imports might reach in the absence of adequate policy measures.[27]

The key features of the plan were to be:

1. Conservation and fuel efficiency, the plan's cornerstone. The annual growth rate of total energy demand would be held to below 2%, gasoline consumption in 1985 should be 10% below its current level, 90% of existing homes and all new buildings should be brought up to minimum energy efficiency standards, and 2.5 million homes should use solar energy.

2. Rational pricing and production policies. Prices of controlled natural gas would be increased to $1.75/mcf. Intrastate gas would be brought under federal regulation. Domestic crude oil prices paid by refiners would be raised to the world level by means of a crude oil equalization tax (COET), making the existing entitlements program unnecessary. Rates charged by electric utilities would be altered to reflect costs as closely as practicable, including seasonal and time of day differentials.

3. Reasonably certain and stable government policies.

4. Substitution of abundant energy resources for those in short supply. This would entail large scale conversion by industry and utilities from oil and gas to coal, consumption of which would be increased by two-thirds in 1985. At the same time, strong efforts would be made to maintain and improve environmental quality, with the aid of improved coal utilization technology and enactment of a national strip mining law. Growth of conventional nuclear power would be encouraged but construction of the breeder reactor would be cancelled.

5. Accelerated development and application of nonconventional resources. Tax credits would be made available for use of solar hot water and space heating. Intangible drilling cost deductions would be extended to geothermal exploration. A wide array of research, development and demonstration projects would be supported by federal funding.

Even before the political reaction to the Carter plan became clear, knowledgeable students of the energy scene voiced serious doubts over whether the plan's objectives were realistic. Their doubts centered around the continued regulation of natural gas prices and its extension to the intrastate market; disposition of receipts from the proposed COET on crude oil, which would be rebated to the public rather than channeled to energy supply development; and the major obstacles to the attainment of the coal expansion target, including air quality standards, a tougher strip mining law, and periodic labor problems. For these reasons, not only private analysts[28] but public agencies with independent judgment[29] doubted that the 1985 oil import objective could be reached. After exceeding an average of 8 million b/d in 1977, the consensus among industry forecasters now appears to be that the U.S. will do well to hold 1985 imports in a range of 10 to 11 million b/d.[30]

In addition, several Carter Plan features have been rejected outright by Congress—a tax-rebate proposal for automobiles and a standby excise tax on gasoline to come into force if consumption did not decline—while others have been seriously weakened, e.g., the coal conversion proposal. A full year after its submission to Congress, the plan is still blocked because of controversy over natural gas policy. A reasonable compromise on this issue, providing for phased decontrol over a number of years, may still emerge, but prospects for letting crude oil prices move toward world levels with or without a tax, are very uncertain. Meanwhile rising oil import costs are a major factor in U.S. trade and payments deficits of unprecedented magnitude and in the continuing deterioration of the dollar against most other currencies. In contrast to Canada, therefore, the United States still has quite a distance to go to put its energy house in an order appropriate to the conditions in which it is having to operate.

# Recent Areas of Cooperation

The United States, while trying to reconcile internal conflicts impeding the formation of a viable energy policy, has
had to cope with additional problems stemming from the
prospect that Canada's resources could no longer be expected
to ease U.S. dependence on imports from the OPEC block.
In fact, the virtual elimination of Canadian oil exports has
posed serious additional difficulties for U.S. oil consumers
(and their suppliers) in the northern tier of states. That the
adjustment process to the new realities has been painful and
has given rise to repeated misunderstandings is scarcely sur-
prising, but a period of shattered illusions has now been replaced by a renewed era of cooperation, though on a greatly
reduced scale. Grandiose dreams of unified energy policies, or
even a common North American energy market, have been
replaced by consideration of individual issues, projects or exchange opportunities which hold promise of mutually beneficial returns to both countries. (For a chronological list of recent events, see Appendix E.)

## The Pipeline Treaty

The first such issue has been the status of existing or future
pipelines crossing the territory of one of the countries with
supplies destined for the other. Lack of any binding agreement that would guarantee an unimpeded flow of materials
through such facilities has constituted a source of periodic
friction between the two countries. It gave rise to the demand

during the Arab oil embargo that the flow of oil through the Portland-Montreal pipeline be stopped. It also was a factor in the debate over whether to build an all-American route to transport North Slope crude oil to the lower 48 states or whether the United States should work with Canada on an overland route directly to the Midwest (though this was hardly the most critical aspect, given the emergency circumstances then prevailing).

Both countries have a strong self-interest in such an agreement. The United States could scarcely consider an overland pipeline for transporting Alaskan gas to U.S. markets unless binding assurances against interference and discriminatory treatment were provided. In the absence of a firm international agreement, the gas pipeline decision would have gone by default to the all-American El Paso proposal, regardless of other merits or drawbacks. Canada, for its part, sought assurances covering not only the Portland-Montreal crude oil line but its Interprovincial Pipeline, which crosses Wisconsin and upper Michigan on its way to eastern Canada. A mutually acceptable agreement was signed by the President and the Prime Minister in January, 1977 and took effect later that year, following ratification by the Senate and House of Commons.[1] Its existence permitted the U.S. State Department to conclude that it saw no special problems in working with Canada on a gas pipeline, and the U.S. Department of Defense to consider the overland pipeline proposals on a par with the El Paso plan from a security point of view.[2]

### Inland Movement of Alaskan Crude

The decision made late in 1973 to transport North Slope crude to the south coast of Alaska and thence by tanker did not solve completely the logistical problems of moving Alaskan oil to U.S. refineries which need it and can process it. Congress wrote into the pipeline legislation a prohibition against exports (Japan would have been a potential customer) since this would not have reduced direct U.S. dependence on imports (even though reliance by western consuming nations on OPEC exports would have been cut). The West Coast can absorb only about half of current North Slope production (550 tb/d of 1.1 mmb/d) because refineries are not equipped to run crude with significant sulfur content and produce finished products that conform to California's very strict air quality standards.[3] Tankers that can move the oil through the Panama Canal to the Gulf Coast, where refineries could process it, are scarce and the shipping cost is high. What is required is one or more west-to-east pipelines which could move the oil to the crude-short Middle West. Of greatest urgency is an alternative access route to crude for refineries along the Northern Tier whose Canadian supply source is being eliminated or sharply reduced.

Four pipeline proposals to accomplish this have been considered and have met with various degrees of success. Farthest along the complex path of regulatory approvals is the one prepared by Sohio Oil Company. Its route would receive crude oil at Long Beach, California and move it east, through a combination of newly constructed and converted natural gas lines, to Midland, Texas, where it would link up with existing crude oil lines running to the Middle West. Another all-American project is that put forward by Northern Tier Pipeline Company, which would entail the construction of an entirely new line from Port Angeles, Washington, to refineries in the states bordering Canada. This proposal has been held in abeyance pending decisions on two alternative northern routes. These would have used all or portions of existing lines and, therefore, would have been less expensive and time consuming to build; both involved cooperation with Canada. One would have required reversal of the Trans Mountain Pipeline, built to move crude oil from Edmonton, Alberta to refineries in the Puget Sound region on both sides of the border, but which has recently been operating well below capacity because of reduced Canadian exports. From Edmonton, the crude would have been shipped to U.S. refineries via the Interprovincial Pipeline. This project had to be withdrawn when Congress prohibited any expansion of the Cherry Point, Washington, port facilities.[4] The other, which called for construction of a new line from Kitimat, British Columbia to Edmonton, was rejected by the Canadian government on environmental grounds.[5]

Problems with these two proposals and the long lead time required to plan and complete a brand new facility like Northern Tier have left some U.S. refineries that operate on Canadian crude, e.g., in Montana and Minnesota, with few alternatives. U.S. pipelines running north from the Gulf of Mexico have little excess capacity and cannot reach out of the way locations in the Northern Plains. Most refineries cannot process the heavy Canadian crudes which are still available. Other options require special accommodation by Canada, either delayed export reductions or some form of swapping. One proposal involves exchanging Canadian crude destined for Northern Tier refineries in return for additional imports into Montreal (via the Portland Pipeline). This plan was initially rejected by Canada because it would cut into the flow of Canadian crude east and endanger the profitability of the Toronto-Montreal line segment.[6] Another possibility discussed between the two countries is "time swaps," i.e., a trade of currently available Canadian crude against U.S. (presumably Alaskan) oil later. The lack of firm assurances as to when and how "repayment" would be possible has presented an obstacle to this alternative. However, the Canadian government subsequently has been reported to be prepared to consider such swaps and also to have reversed its previous objections to trading Canadian for foreign crude.[7] Canada appears willing to do more than voice its sympathy for consumers south of the border who have been severed from their established crude supply connections.

### The Alaskan Gas Route

By far the largest recent energy trade issue involving the United States and Canada has been the selection of the route for moving natural gas from the North Slope of Alaska to the lower 48 states. Three competing proposals were considered. The first, and most thoroughly prepared, was that of the

Alaskan Arctic Gas group. It was to run parallel to the Beaufort Sea to the Mackenzie Delta, then south up the Mackenzie and on to Caroline Junction, Alberta, where it would have divided into two legs, one running southeast to the Chicago region and the other southwest to the San Francisco area. The line, 30 to 48 inches in size, would have had a total length of about 4,500 miles. It was sponsored by 16 American and Canadian companies, including gas producers, transmitters and distributors. It would have been capable of moving at least 2.2 billion cubic feet per day (bcfd) of Alaskan and Canadian gas to major markets in both countries. Cost was estimated at $6.73 billion (in 1975 dollars, U.S. share only).[8]

The major competing proposal for quite some time was an all-American route proposed by El Paso Natural Gas Company. This was to consist of a pipeline paralleling the Alaskan oil line to the south coast at Gravina Point, near Valdez, where the gas would have been liquefied and put on cryogenic tankers. It was to be shipped to Point Conception, north of Los Angeles, where it would have been unloaded, regasified, and moved partly through existing pipeline networks and partly to major markets in the Midwest and East by displacement. Capacity was to be 2.1 bcfd and estimated cost $6.57 billion (in 1975 dollars). Since this facility would not have linked up with Canada, a Canadian group submitted an all-Canadian proposal, Maple Leaf, for moving Delta gas to southern Alberta.[9]

Late in the proceedings a third option, originally called the Alcan project and now renamed Northwest, was submitted and considered. It proposed to follow the Alaskan oil line part way, to the Fairbanks region, and then move southeast parallel to the Alcan Highway to the James River Junction in Alberta. From there, gas moving to the eastern United States would be transported to Monchy, Saskatchewan, and gas destined for the western United States to Kingsgate, British Columbia. The principal sponsors of this proposal were Northwest Pipeline Corp. of Salt Lake City and several Canadian transmission companies, including Foothills Pipe Lines, Westcoast Transmission and Alberta Gas Trunk Line. It was to consist of 4,800 miles of 48 and 42 inch diameter pipe. Its capacity would be at least 2.2 bcfd and estimated cost $6.75 billion (in 1975 dollars).[10]

The decision making process, which proceeded simultaneously in both countries, was complex. It involved specialized energy agencies like the U.S. Federal Power Commission and Canada's National Energy Board, an interdepartmental task force on the U.S. side, the chief executives and their advisers, and both countries' legislatures. Aspects covered ranged from technical feasibility to environmental impact, effects on native tribes, national security, cost, and financial feasibility. The process began in March 1974, with the filing of the first applications and is still continuing on such issues as specification of the line, pricing principles, and financial arrangements.

Decisions made by one country necessarily limited the remaining options and thus affected the determinations of the other. The first ruling came on February 1, 1977, when the Administrative Law Judge hearing the case before the Federal Power Commission recommended approval of the Alaskan Arctic Gas project, terming it superior to both competitors with respect to timing, cost and environmental impact.[11] Three months later, the full commission found an overland pipeline route superior to El Paso's pipeline-tanker combination on the basis of reliability, efficiency and environmental impact. It divided evenly on whether to recommend the Arctic Gas or the Northwest proposal, however, stating that it lacked adequate information "as well as an understanding of the intentions of the Government of Canada."[12] The El Paso proposal appeared to be dead, unless Canada refused permission for any line carrying Alaskan gas to cross its territory.

Only a week later, the Canadian Commission of Inquiry studying the impact of pipeline construction on the northern territories, headed by Justice Thomas Berger, recommended a 10-year delay in building a line through the Mackenzie Valley. It based its findings on the fear that such a line would inflict serious environmental damage on the region and cause critical social and economic problems for its native population.[13] Finally, on July 4, the National Energy Board denied the application of Canadian Arctic Gas on the basis of incompatible time constraints (urgent need for a facility to move Alaskan gas versus time needed to resolve socio-economic concerns) and unacceptable environmental impacts. Instead, it favored the application of Foothills (Yukon), the Canadian segment of the Northwest project, subject to certain conditions. Chief among these were an alteration in the line's route to run it by Dawson City, Yukon, nearer to Mackenzie Delta gas fields; linkage of a lateral running from the delta along the Dempster Highway with the main line by January 1, 1984; and agreeing to pay up to $200 million in socio-economic costs incurred by the project north of the 60th parallel.[14]

In mid-August, the Canadian cabinet endorsed these recommendations and authorized negotiations with the United States aimed at minimizing adverse socio-economic and environmental impacts and protecting claims of the native population. Extensive discussions followed during the next several weeks on both the cabinet and subcabinet levels. President Carter postponed his original decision date, September 1, pending complete agreement with Canada on major issues. The principal American objections concerned the extra cost imposed on Alaskan gas customers as a result of the diversion, the magnitude of socio-economic costs, and the desire for an "all events" tariff.[15] The option of shifting to the El Paso project, which remained alive, was considered by some a strong bargaining weapon in the hands of U.S. negotiators.[16]

The final outcome was a compromise including a shorter diversion than Canada had proposed and repayment of the damage fund from taxes collected by the Yukon Territory. In turn, the U.S. Government agreed to share in the extra cost of transporting delta gas, when and if it was developed, to compensate for the greater distance to the link-up with the main Northwest line. Following cabinet approval of these terms, the President and Prime Minister signed the agreement in early September. Congressional approval followed in November and Canadian legislative approval (of the Canadian segment) in April, 1978.

The struggle for the Alaskan gas transmission rights was

protracted and intense. Even before the entry of the Northwest group's proposal, major lobbying and publicity cam-
paigns were carried on by both overland and land-sea propo-
nents. El Paso argued strongly for the merits of an all-U.S.
project, which would create jobs for the country's construction workers and seamen and orders for its steel mills and
shipyards. The all-pipeline advocates stressed the greater
safety of an overland route, less environmental impact and
lower cost. Estimates provided at the time of Presidential approval indicated a cost saving of 30 cents a thousand cubic
feet (mcf) for the final pipeline route over the El Paso proposal (79 cents vs. $1.09).[17] Such comparisons should be
considered with great reservation. They do not allow for cost
escalation, which in recent years has been huge for virtually
all large construction projects[18] and unbelievable for some,
notably the Alaskan oil pipeline. In the view of some experts,
the final pipeline tariff will be several times the estimates provided by the company. Unless the cost of Alaskan gas were
"rolled in" or combined with that of lower cost supplies, customers would be extremely hard to find.[19] In such an event,
financing could not be obtained and the line would never be
built.

This view may be extreme, if only because a gas line does
not pose the same problems as an oil line, e.g., of impacting
on the delicate environment of the far north. No firm judgment of the benefits and costs of the pipeline can be formed,
however, until the remaining questions concerning pricing,
tariffs, financing, etc. are resolved. Even such technical decisions as what combination of line size and pressure to select
has been highly controversial, since steel mills in the two
countries are not equally capable of providing pipe of different sizes.[20]

From a broader perspective, it is encouraging that the complex and difficult decision process progressed quite smoothly
during the critical period in 1977. Instead of recriminations
and inward turning, there was tough but fair bargaining between the two countries' representatives, carried out in a
business-like atmosphere with due consideration for the other

side's point of view and with reasonable compromise as the final outcome. The turnaround from the failures of a few short years before bodes well for future collaboration on a variety of projects of mutual concern.

## Short-Term Gas Exports

The recently developed surplus of natural gas in western Canada, the continuing gas shortage in the United States and agreement on an overland route for the shipment of Alaskan gas have opened up an opportunity for increased Canadian gas exports to the United States. A source of interim relief has become particularly urgent for California, where supplies for top priority residential and small commercial customers are expected to fall short by the winter of 1980-81 and no new long-term supply source is in prospect until 1983, when liquefied natural gas (LNG) from Indonesia is expected to arrive.[21] Canadian producers, for their part, have come under pressure from "shut-in" wells, which have been capped because their operation is not profitable at current prices. These are beginning to jeopardize the recent exploration boom and threaten to offset the benefits of higher prices and other incentives.[22]

During the unusually severe winter of 1976-77, Canada already had made available limited "emergency exports" to help alleviate shortages in the northeastern United States[23] and seasonal exchanges of Canadian gas for U.S. electricity.[24] Canada was ready to consider various alternatives for enlarging markets for its gas. One option was an expansion of gas flows to eastern Canada; this would have required a change in the policy of subsidizing imported oil, which kept energy prices there too low for Canadian gas to be competitive.[25] Another was a "time swap" arrangement with the United States, under which Canada would reserve the right to be "repaid" for its additional gas exports with equivalent volumes of North Slope gas once this became available. Should the Canadian gas surplus continue, the option presumably would not be exercised.

The subject of increased Canadian gas exports constituted one of several energy related topics discussed between the two governments in the fall of 1977. Canada reportedly stressed the priority it attached to meeting the goal of holding oil imports in 1985 to one-third of total demand and the possibility that gas consumption in the East might have to be greatly expanded to reach this target.[26] A special complication was the attitude of the western provinces, which play a very considerable role in resource export decisions. Alberta attempted to tie increased gas exports to trade concessions on chemicals and agricultural products.[27] British Columbia hesitated to approve additional exports of Alberta gas moving across its territory for fear of losing future markets for its own gas.[28] These difficulties were apparently overcome by early 1978, when the NEB reported it was ready to approve the accelerated construction of both the eastern and western legs of the Northwest Alaska Pipeline and the exportation of additional gas by November 1, 1980.[29] An important factor in the picture no doubt has been the increasing realization that the prospect of a Canadian gas shortage any time during the 1980s has greatly diminished with the discovery of important new deposits in Alberta and British Columbia, which could rival those of the North Slope.[30]

## Other Common Energy Issues

Recent discussions between officials of the two countries have covered a wide range of specific energy and environmental issues. In October, 1976, subcabinet level talks were conducted on a series of oil and gas related topics.[31] In February, 1977, the President and the Prime Minister discussed cooperation on over 15 environmental problems, some of them energy based.[32] In midsummer 1977, the outstanding issues were reported to have been reduced to six or seven, and Canada had submitted final positions on all of them.[33] Three months later, the U.S. Ambassador to Ottawa was said to be discussing a "comprehensive bilateral treaty" which would involve recognition of "Canada's special position" as the leading trading partner of the United States. In the energy area, the United States was reported to be prepared to recognize trade as a "two-way street" and to give assurances that exports of U.S. coal to Canada would continue, in exchange for Canadian assurances on continuing exports of gas and certain chemical feedstocks. Also mentioned were potential joint efforts to develop oil sands and shale oil, and the construction of joint oil ports.[34] In early 1978, talks between the Prime Minister and the Vice President led to their agreement to encourage closer energy cooperation in such areas as short term gas shipments, oil export swaps, additional electricity exchanges, and strategic oil storage. The latter would entail the joint use of abandoned coal mines and other suitable caverns in Nova Scotia and Newfoundland as part of the U.S. strategic oil reserve, with the U.S. share of the stored oil earmarked for emergency use in New England.[35]

Still another collaborative venture is a proposal by Tenneco Pipeline Company to construct a terminal and vaporization facility at St. John, New Brunswick for processing Algerian liquid natural gas. The bulk of this gas would be used to supplement the company's diminishing supplies for markets in New England and the mid-Atlantic states. Alternative terminal sites in Rhode Island and Maine were considered not viable because of local opposition. The project has been approved by the National Energy Board and the Federal Energy Regulatory Commission and is awaiting action by the U.S. Energy Regulatory Agency.[36]

# 8
# Some Lessons

U.S.-Canadian energy trade relations have recently passed through a difficult period. Painful adjustments to new realities were forced on both countries as the previous era of smooth and normal commercial relationships encountered almost continuous strains in the face of radical new situations. The adjustments led each country to follow a path independent from the other, chosen in its own best interests, without consultation or even prior notification of the trading partner. Regardless of justification, such actions at times have given the appearance to the partner of constituting a deliberate slap in the face.

Fortunately, there are strong indications that the recent regrettable experience has run its course and that apparent suspicions of one another's motives will be a thing of the past. The conclusion of the pipeline treaty, the selection of an overland route for Alaskan gas and other recent examples of collaboration constitute proof that issues affecting the two nations can be examined on their merits, by each side singly and jointly, and the benefits and drawbacks of mutual collaboration versus going-it-alone determined case by case. Where a joint project offers few advantages, there is no reason it should be given preference over a "national" alternative confined to one country's territory. Proposals that are clearly superior on economic, environmental or other grounds need not be cast aside just because they happen to be trans-national.

No doubt, cases will arise in which the two countries will agree to disagree. No matter what the ultimate decision in any given situation, one may hope that every effort will be made by both parties to explore and fully comprehend the other's viewpoint, needs and constraints. In no case should decisions be cast in a light which would give unnecessary offense to the other country. In every instance affecting the partner's interests, it is essential that prior exchange of information and close consultation occur at various stages of the decision process, as was the case in the selection of the Alaskan gas line.

After a number of decades of relative continental tranquility, the nations sharing North America currently are facing major internal problems, though of a different nature. Canada's are political in origin: how to preserve and strengthen the foundations of nationhood in the face of strong separatist pressures. Adverse economic consequences have been inevitable. Mexico's are primarily socio-economic: how to satisfy the aspirations of its underprivileged classes without weakening incentives for domestic and foreign investors, whose contribution is essential to continued national progress. The United States faces a series of its own complex issues: the inflation dilemma, decay of the cities, energy-and-environmental conflicts, to name a few. One would hope that in grappling with their internal problems, the countries will take into account each others' needs and sensitivities, so that in the future their trade relationships can develop beneficially, devoid of the acrimony of recent years. Proximity always carries with it a measure of friction but with the recent history of U.S.-Canadian energy trade relations as a useful lesson, irritations need not become festering sores.

# Notes

## Chapter 2

1. *Reserves of Crude Oil, Natural Gas Liquids and Natural Gas in the United States and Canada as of December 31* (annual), 1975, pp. 2, 226, 228. The Prudhoe Bay field was discovered in 1968 and its reserves were added to the published figures in 1970.

2. Among the dissenters, who viewed potential U.S. reserves much more conservatively than most, was King Hubbert, senior geologist with the U.S. Geological Survey. Official estimates recently have been scaled sharply downward from earlier figures.

3. Cabinet Task Force on Oil Import Control, *The Oil Import Question,* February 1970. The Task Force majority recommended that imports from Eastern Hemisphere sources be restricted to 10% of domestic demand (pp. 98-99) but that Western Hemisphere sources have restricted access to U.S. markets.

4. Ministry of Energy, Mines and Resources, *An Energy Policy for Canada–Phase I,* Vol. I, Analysis, 1973, p. 91.

5. *Ibid.* (Vol. II, p. 32) estimated recoverable oil sands at 300.9 billion barrels and Alberta heavy oil at 30 billion barrels.

6. *Ibid.,* Vol. I, pp. 81-84.

7. Proved reserves of Canadian crude and natural gas liquids declined in 1970 for the first time in over 20 years and natural gas reserves declined in 1972. *Reserves of Crude Oil, Natural Gas Liquids and Natural Gas in the United States and Canada as of December 31* (1975).

8. See Chapter 3 for a discussion of U.S.-Canadian trade in coal, electricity, and uranium.

9. For a brief history of the Canadian oil and gas industries, see Appendix E.

10. The National Energy Board grants export licenses for gas only

for quantities shown to be surplus to Canadian domestic requirements, determined on the basis of 25 times demands in the fourth year (25 A4 formula).

11. An earlier estimate by the National Energy Board (*Energy Supply and Demand in Canada and Export Demand for Canadian Energy, 1966 to 1990,* 1969) projected petroleum exports in 1985 at 1.97-2.5 million b/d and gas available for export at 1.449-3.7 tcf. See pp. 55-56, 63-64.

12. National Petroleum Council Case II assumed a 3.5% annual increase in oil and gas drilling and a high projection of oil and gas discovered per foot drilled.

13. The estimates envisage Canadian Atlantic offshore and Mackenzie Delta supplies to become available by 1980 and Beaufort Sea offshore supplies by 1985. See National Petroleum Council, *U.S. Energy Outlook* (December 1972), p. 267.

14. NPC's Oil Supply Task Group projected the flow of frontier oil supplies to begin by 1980 and to reach 1.2 MM b/d by 1985. See its *Initial Appraisal,* p. 26.

### Chapter 3

1. Present estimates place Canadian coal resources at about 120 billion tons, of which 99% are located in Saskatchewan, Alberta, and British Columbia. See Ministry of Energy, Mines and Resources, *An Energy Policy for Canada–Phase I,* Vol. I, p. 82 and Vol. II, p. 264. According to government sources only 4% of this total is currently recoverable, primarily by stripping. The remainder is located in inaccessible areas where mining is difficult or would require underground mining techniques. See *Coal and Canada-U.S. Energy Relations,* Canadian-American Committee (1976), p. 37.

2. Alberta recently declared that it will no longer authorize the use of natural gas to produce methanol, so that in the future this product will have to be derived from coal. *The Oil Daily,* August 11, 1976.

3. Negotiations were reported under way for shipments starting as early as 1977 but important issues, including a price competitive with supplies from the United States, had not yet been agreed upon. *The Oil Daily,* July 24, 1975.

4. See discussion in Richard L. Gordon, *Coal and Canada-U.S. Energy Relations* (Canadian-American Committee, Montreal, 1976), p. 68.

5. *Vancouver Sun,* August 18, 1975; *The Oil Daily,* June 23, July 8 and November 8, 1976.

6. National Energy Board, *Annual Report, 1975,* p. 22 and Edison Electric Institute, *Statistical Year Book* for 1974, Table 3S.

7. National Energy Board, *op. cit.,* 1974, pp. 22-23 and 1975, p. 23.

8. *Ibid.,* pp. 22, 24 and 22-23.

9. Except in Alberta, all Canadian hydroelectric operations are government monopolies, whose policy it is to sell power at cost (generally average cost).

10. Larrett Higgins, "Electricity and Canadian Policy," in E.W. Erickson and L. Waverman, *The Energy Question: An International Failure of Policy,* Vol. 2, North America (1974), pp. 182-185.

11. Private correspondence by Mr. Hugh L. Keenleyside, former Chairman of the British Columbia Hydro and Power Authority dated February 11 and May 19, 1977, expanding on an article which appeared in the *Victoria Colonist* (Victoria, B.C.), December 13, 1974.

12. Thorium is another fissionable material which may be used, under alternative technologies, as a raw material for generating nuclear power.

13. Ministry of Energy, Mines and Resources, "1975 Assessment of Canada's Uranium Supply and Demand" (June 1976). The report, prepared by a Uranium Resource Appraisal Group, weights measured resources by 1.0, indicated resources by 0.8 and inferred resources by 0.7, to allow for uncertainty.

14. U.S. uranium reserves in 1975 were estimated by the Energy Research and Development Administration at 600,000 tons $U_3O_8$. Probable resources were given as 1,140,000 tons; possible as 1,340,000 tons and speculative resources as 410,000 tons. These are for forward costs to $30 per pound, which is similar to the more recent Canadian estimates of up to $40 a pound because of recent sharp price increases. See Federal Energy Administration, *1976 National Energy Outlook,* p. 256.

15. The Federal Energy Administration, in its 1976 *Outlook* (p. 36) estimated U.S. costs of nuclear power in base load operations at 18 mills/KwH. Canada's recent experience is reported on the order of 10 mills/KwH. This relationship reflects chiefly the fact that the Canadian reactor uses natural rather than enriched uranium, thus achieving lower fuel costs, which offset somewhat greater capital costs.

16. Assuming an average load factor of 80%. The ministry shows a range between low and high estimates for 1985 of 12,800 to 17,800 mw. This compares with 55,500 to 61,900 mw for hydro power. See Ministry of Energy, Mines and Resources, *An Energy Strategy for Canada,* p. 68.

17. Canada has signed agreements to provide nuclear technology

and supplies with South Korea, Argentina and Finland. Agreements were reported being negotiated with Japan and a number of European countries. Shipments to the United States, which until recently prohibited imports of uranium, to date have been small. Canada has insisted on strict safeguards against the danger of misuse since India exploded a nuclear device made from materials obtained from its Canadian built reactor. The government was heavily criticized for permitting exports to some countries which are not parties to the nuclear non-proliferation treaty (*Toronto Globe and Mail,* April 23, 1976).

18. Including two Energy Research and Development Administration (ERDA)-owned units. See ERDA Press Release No. 76-66, August 3, 1976.

19. *The 1976 National Energy Outlook* (p. 36) projects actual capacity expected in 1985 at 142,000 mw. This represents a sizable reduction from earlier estimates, e.g., 204,000 mw used by the Federal Energy Administration in its late 1974 report.

20. In 1975 dollars ($40 a pound in 1976 dollars). A load factor of 70% is assumed for U.S. reactors (against one of 80% for Canadian plants). Backup supply assumptions of 30-year $U_3O_8$ requirements are identical.

21. In connection with a recent antitrust suit by Westinghouse, the Canadian Government reportedly has admitted the existence, and even active encouragement, of a uranium cartel. This, however, dates to the early 1970s, when world uranium prices were depressed. The U.S. market closed to foreign producers, and U.S. firms were competing in export markets. With the sharp increases in uranium prices, following those of oil and other energy sources, concerted price action is said to have ceased (*Wall Street Journal,* September 23, 1976).

**Chapter 4**

1. Eric C. Sievwright has traced the "Continental Energy Concept" back to 1948. See "A Continental Energy Policy—Future Fact or Fiction?" (American Institute of Mining Engineers paper, New York City, March 1, 1971, p. 13).

2. Leonard Waverman, "The Reluctant Bride: Canadian and American Energy Relations," in Edward W. Erikson and Leonard Waverman (ed.), *The Energy Question in International Failure of Policy, Volume 2, North America* (University of Toronto Press, 1974), p. 218.

3. The disadvantage of Canadian crude in Montreal at the time was estimated at 25-35 cents/barrel. See J.G. Debanne, "Oil and Canadian

Policy," in Erickson andWaverman, *op. cit.*, p. 130. The Canadian Independent Producers Association was turned down by the federal government as late as June 1969 in its bid to extend the Interprovincial Pipeline to Montreal. See Carl Nickel, "A North American Cooperative Energy Policy," in J. Alex Murray (ed.), *North American Energy in Perspective,* Proceedings of the 16th University of Windsor Seminar on Canadian American Relations, November 14-15, 1969 (University of Windsor, 1975), p. 124.

4. Ministry of Energy, Mines and Resources, *An Energy Policy for Canada,* Vol. II, pp. 313-315. Eastern Canadian consumers did not reap the full benefit of the policy until 1970, when the Province of Quebec objected to the major oil importers' use of official posted crude oil prices rather than competitive market prices. The U.S. and Canadian governments exchanged secret correspondence on the issue of Venezuelan oil shipments to eastern Canada, apparently because the Venezuelan and the major international oil companies were anxious to have continued access to the Canadian market. See Debanne, *op. cit.,* pp. 130-32.

5. Kenneth W. Dam, *Implementation of Import Quotas: The Case of Oil* (Washington, Brookings Institution, 1971), p. 29. Imports into the West Coast (Petroleum Administration for Defense District V) were determined by deducting available domestic supplies from total demand.

6. Leonard Waverman, *Natural Gas and National Policy* (Toronto, University of Toronto Press, 1973), pp. 15-17. The author interprets the decision to build an all-Canadian line as resting on the notion that east-west (or west-east) transport facilities should serve as instruments of Canadian unification, although he questions the applicability of this concept to a gas pipeline (as distinct from, say, a railway). In rejecting an application for a second gas line, this one to cross U.S. territory, Prime Minister Lester Pearson stated, on August 25, 1966: "The government does not believe it is to be in Canada's best interest that the future development of facilities for bringing western gas to its eastern Canadian market should be located outside Canadian jurisdiction and subject to detailed regulation under the laws of the United States which are naturally designed to protect the interests of the United States citizens." (*Ibid.,* p. 18) The Canadian Cabinet later reversed this decision and approved the line.

7. *National Energy Board Annual Reports.*

8. Dam, *op. cit.,* p. 30.

9. Debanne, *op. cit.,* p. 134.

10. *The Oil Import Question,* pp. 136-139. There was a question as

to whether a tariff alone would have been able to hold Eastern Hemisphere imports to the level of 10% of domestic demand recommended on national security grounds, since the ability of Western Hemisphere sources to expand production was limited. See National Petroleum Council, *U.S. Energy Outlook, An Initial Appraisal,* Vol. I, p. 28.

11. The Cabinet Task Force recommended that oil import quotas be abandoned in favor of a set of tariffs. See *The Oil Import Question,* pp. 134-136.

12. One of every four Canadians visits the United States in an average year. Defense collaboration has included participation in the North American Air Defense (NORAD) and membership in the North Atlantic Treaty Organization (NATO).

13. Thomas L. Powrie and Bruce W. Wilkinson, "Canadian Trade Patterns and Commercial Policy," in L.H. Officer and L.B. Smith (ed.), *Issues in Canadian Economics* (McGraw-Hill, 1975), p. 60.

14. Foreign owned companies, predominantly U.S. corporations, controlled 74% of investment in Canadian oil and gas operations in 1967. See A.E. Safanian, "Issues Raised by Foreign Direct Investment in Canada," in Officer and Smith, *op. cit.,* p. 80.

15. Charles J. Cicchetti, *Alaskan Oil, Alternative Routes and Markets* (Resources for the Future, 1972), pp. 56-57.

16. John Lichtblau, in National Planning Association, *Looking Ahead* (November 1971).

17. H.S. Houthakker stated that unrestricted oil imports from Canada would not be consistent with present U.S. oil policy "unless a concerted policy is developed with respect to emergency supplies for Eastern Canada (remarks at the University of Calgary) and the University of Alberta, April 1 and 2, 1971).

18. By 1970, when the reserve-to-production ratio for Canadian natural gas had fallen below 30, the Canadian Government denied applications for additional gas exports.

19. The volume of crude oil which the Alaska pipeline is designed to deliver at full capacity (2.0 million b/d) exceeds total oil imports into Petroleum Administration for Defense District V. Several alternative means for moving the surplus Alaskan crude oil inland are currently under study. See Staff analysis of U.S. Senate Committee on Interior and Insular Affairs, *The Trans-Alaska Pipeline and West Coast Petroleum Supply,* 1977-1982, 93d Congress, 2d Session, Serial Number 93-51 (92-86), pp. 13-14.

20. Cicchetti, *op. cit.,* p. 56.

21. Paul G. Bradley, *et al.,* "United States and Canadian Trade in Energy Resources: Issues and Alternatives," Background Paper for a

U.S.-Canadian Energy Conference, Vancouver, B.C., October 1972, pp. 48-50.

22. *Ibid.*, pp. 50-51.

23. Dam, *op. cit.*, pp. 30-31.

24. Ministry of Energy, Mines and Resources, *op. cit.*, Vol. II, p. 307.

25. Judith Maxwell, *Energy from the Arctic: Facts and Issues*, Canadian-American Committee (November 1973), pp. 38-39.

26. The surcharge was imposed unilaterally on imports from all sources. It was removed in January 1972, following the Washington conference agreement on a new system of exchange rates.

27. Quotas on oil imports were officially removed on April 18, 1973.

28. Deputy Minister Jack Austin denied that the action constituted a breach of contract since negotiations were conducted with the affected parties. See *Proceedings of the 68th Annual Meeting of the American Society of International Law*, pp. 88-89.

29. *Ibid.*, pp. 89-90.

30. National Energy Board, *1973 Annual Report.*

31. National Energy Board, *1974 Annual Report*, p. 14.

32. *The Oil Daily*, October 25 and December 21, 1973. Thirty percent of the planned fourth quarter oil imports into Canada originated with Arab countries, chiefly Saudi Arabia and the Trucial states. See "Current Canadian Oil Supply and Demand Fact Sheet" accompanying statement by Minister for Energy Donald S. Macdonald, November 1, 1973.

33. *The Oil Daily*, November 23, 1973. Shipments from Vancouver via the Panama Canal began in mid-November and ran at about 50,000 b/d, or half of the deficit of eastern refiners.

34. John Saywell (ed.), *Canadian Annual Review of Politics and Public Affairs, 1973*, University of Toronto Press, pp. 328-330.

**Chapter 5**

1. Powrie and Wilkinson, *op. cit.*, p. 63.

2. See Chapter 2.

3. For an account of the Waffle group position, see James Laxer, *The Energy Poker Game, The Politics of the Continental Resources* (New Press, Toronto, 1970).

4. Richard Rohmer, *Ultimatum* (Erwin Clarke, Toronto, 1973).

5. American publications, including *Time* and *Readers Digest*, recently were forced to choose between issuing Canadian versions or ceasing sales in Canada.

6. For an example of this view, see Mel Hurtig in J. Alex Murray,

*op. cit.,* pp. 140-153. For a more scholarly treatment, consult the writings of Professor Milton Moore of the University of British Columbia.

7. Gunter Schramm, "The Resource-Industry Problem," in Officer and Smith, *op. cit.,* pp. 117-125.

8. Powrie and Wilkinson, *op. cit.,* pp. 67-68.

9. Leonard Waverman, "Energy in Canada, A Question of Economic Rents," in Officer and Smith, *op. cit.,* pp. 135-149.

10. The point was made by several participants at the October 1972 conference on U.S.-Canadian energy trade.

11. Note the similarity to the situation in Scotland, where environmentalists have been unable to block development of facilities supporting North Sea petroleum operations but must seek compromises and trade-offs.

12. Benefit-cost comparisons are helpful in decision-making even though the results are usually indicative rather than conclusive, e.g., because some costs (or benefits) are not readily quantifiable.

13. Address by H.S. Houthakker, *loc. cit.*

14. Address of Minister for Energy Donald S. Macdonald to the Royal Society of Canada Symposium on Energy Resources, October 16, 1973.

15. September, 1971 meeting with U.S. delegation headed by Secretary of the Treasury John S. Connally.

16. Visit to Ottawa, April 1972. President Nixon aroused Canadian resentment by stating (incorrectly) that Canada was the U.S.' second best customer, after Japan.

17. Canadian-American Committee, *op. cit.,* p. 12.

18. This agreement has benefited both partners by permitting greater specialization in production. Motor vehicles and parts were Canada's largest export category.

19. Saywell, *op. cit.,* p. 323.

20. The same view was held of other energy producers, e.g., the British, Norwegians, and even Alaskans, who insisted on maximum proceeds from exports of oil and gas.

21. National Energy Board, *op. cit.,* p. 15.

22. Meeting with Minister for Energy Donald S. Macdonald, January 1974.

23. Secretary of the Treasury William E. Simon had extensive training in economics and a career in banking.

24. Secretary of State Henry Kissinger reportedly was one such official.

25. H.R. Haldeman, *The Ends of Power* (Time Books, 1978).

26. Judith Maxwell in J. Alex Murray, *op. cit.*, p. 13.

27. Remarks by Julius L. Katz, Deputy Assistant Secretary of State for International Resources and Food Policy, in American Society of International Law, *loc. cit.*, p. 84.

28. See Chapter 2, Tables 1, 2 and 3.

29. A different example of divergent interests (and policies) is the case of uranium, where Canada admittedly participated in a cartel-type price fixing arrangement in 1972-73. This was deemed necessary in the face of very low world prices and Canadian dependence on export markets. The United States, with its large domestic outlets, provided subsidies for uranium producers rather than permitting price fixing, which is illegal under U.S. antitrust laws. Canadian policy came to light following disclosure by Westinghouse Electric Corp. of its inability to supply uranium to electric utility customers and the latters' suit on price fixing charges. See *Business Week,* November 1, 1976, pp. 92-97.

## Chapter 6

1. *An Energy Strategy for Canada: Policies for Self-Reliance* (April 27, 1976).

2. *Ibid.* Notes released by Canadian Embassy, Washington, D.C., p. 4.

3. National Energy Board. *Canadian Oil Supply and Requirements* (February 1977).

4. *Ibid.,* p. 6.

5. Imperial Oil Company, *Annual Report 1977,* p. 16.

6. *The Oil and Gas Journal,* January 30, 1978, pp. 87-91.

7. *Ibid.,* March 27, 1978, p. 100.

8. *The Wall Street Journal,* January 31, 1978. Interim terms for frontier exploration were also modified in 1977.

9. *Ibid.,* p. 27.

10. Speech by Minister for Energy Alastair Gillespie, April 27, 1977.

11. *The Oil and Gas Journal,* March 27, 1978, pp. 98-100.

12. NEB, *Canadian Oil Supply and Requirements* (February 1977), Appendix G.

13. The size of the proposed Polar Gas line was reduced from 48 to 42 inches before the application was submitted to the NEB in late 1977. It would have a capacity of 000 mmcfd and require 14-16 tcf backup reserves. According to Panarctic, discoveries total nearly that much, but only the 9.5 tcf discovered on Melville Island may be counted because technical problems may not permit connections across the Arctic Ocean

to other fields until a later time. *The Oil and Gas Journal,* June 27, 1977, p. 81.

14. Delays were recommended by both the Berger and LYSYR inquiries, which studied the socio-economic and environmental impacts of northern pipelines on the Yukon region and its inhabitants. *The Oil and Gas Journal,* May 16, 1977, p. 60 and *The Oil Daily,* August 4, 1977.

15. See Chapter 7, p. 50.

16. *Business Week,* May 30, 1977, pp. 26-27.

17. *The Wall Street Journal,* June 24, 1977.

18. *The Oil and Gas Journal,* July 4, 1977, pp. 42-43.

19. For opposing views, see M.A. Adelman, "Is the Oil Shortage Real?" *Foreign Policy,* Winter 1972-73, pp. 69-107, and James E. Akins, "The Oil Crisis: This Time the Wolf Is Here," *Foreign Affairs,* April 1973, pp. 462-490.

20. Precise arrangements vary. In some countries (e.g., Venezuela) government companies have taken over most of the responsibilities of the previous concessionaires. In others (e.g., Saudi Arabia) the latter continue to market most of the oil produced. However, output is limited and the companies' profit margin slim, so that there is little likelihood of price cuts. See M.A. Adelman, "The Strengths of OPEC," *REF Resources,* Summer 1976.

21. All three of these proposals were included in the 1976 platform of the Democratic Party.

22. The original target for attaining independence was 1980, but this soon changed to the mid-1980s. Also, "independence" was redefined as reduced reliance on imports rather than zero imports.

23. Federal Energy Administration, *Project Independence Report,* November 1974.

24. Federal Energy Administration, *1976 National Energy Outlook,* February 1976, Appendix G, and *1977 National Energy Outlook.* The latter was circulated only in draft form, since it was outdated by the change in administrations in January 1977.

25. Executive Office of the President, Energy Policy and Planning, *The National Energy Plan,* April 29, 1977.

26. *Ibid.,* p. IX.

27. *Ibid.,* p. XIII.

28. Roger F. Naill *et al.,* "Evaluating the National Energy Plan," Technology Review, July-August 1977, John H. Lichtblau, "Can the Goal of the Administration's National Energy Plan Be Met?" August, 1977.

29. See, for example, Congressional Budget Office, President Carter's Energy Proposals; A Perspective Staff Working Paper (June 1977).

30. For an excellent analysis of the shortcomings of the Carter Plan, see Walker J. Mead, "An Economic Appraisal of President Carter's Energy Program," International Institute for Economic Research, Reprint Paper 7 (September 1977).

**Chapter 7**

1. *The Wall Street Journal,* August 4, 1977.

2. *The Oil Daily,* July 5, 1977.

3. *The Oil and Gas Journal,* July 18, 1977, pp. 21-23.

4. *Business Week,* November 28, 1977.

5. *The Wall Street Journal,* February 24, 1978.

6. *Ibid.,* December 15, 1977.

7. *The Oil and Gas Journal,* December 26, 1977, p. 83.

8. Federal Power Commission (FPC), "Alaska Natural Gas Fact Sheet," News Release No. 23112, May 2, 1977.

9. *Ibid.*

10. *Ibid.*

11. FPC News Release No. 22868, February 1, 1977.

12. FPC News Release No. 23113, May 2, 1977.

13. *The Wall Street Journal,* May 10, 1977.

14. National Energy Board, "Fact Sheet Regarding National Energy Board Decision on the Northern Gas Pipeline Applications," July 4, 1977.

15. An "all events" tariff requires customers to continue paying the pipeline even if the flow of gas is reduced or interrupted.

16. *The Wall Street Journal,* September 8, 1977.

17. *Ibid.*

18. Walter J. Mead found that final costs of 12 large construction projects average 2.21 times initial estimates, while the cost of Alyeska was 4.25 times the initial figure. See *Transporting Natural Gas from the Arctic; The Alternative Systems.* American Enterprise Institute for Policy Research (1977), Chapter 6.

19. *The Oil and Gas Journal,* October 10, 1977, p. 62.

20. Canada's selection of the 56-inch, low pressure alternative aroused strong criticism in the United States, where only one steel mill can produce pipe of this size. *The Oil and Gas Journal,* February 27, 1978, pp. 47-48.

21. *The Oil and Gas Journal,* March 20, 1978, p. 38.

22. *Oil Week,* January 16, 1978, p. 58.

23. National Energy Board, *Annual Report 77,* p. 24.

24. Federal Power Commission News Release No. 22887 (February 5, 1977) and No. 22978 (March 3, 1977).

25. *The Oil Daily,* November 4, 1977.

26. *Ibid.,* September 14, 1977.

27. *The Wall Street Journal,* January 18, 1978. U.S. Negotiations reportedly made no commitment on Alberta's demands.

28. *The Oil Daily,* April 1, 1977.

29. *The Oil and Gas Journal,* March 20, 1978, p. 38.

30. *The Wall Street Journal,* January 31, 1978.

31. *The Oil Daily,* October 15, 1976.

32. U.S. State Department Bureau of Public Affairs, *GIST,* "U.S.-Canada Relations," March, 1977.

33. *The Oil Daily,* July 25, 1977.

34. *Ibid.,* October 28, 1977.

35. *The Wall Street Journal,* January 18, 1978.

36. National Energy Board, *Annual Report 77,* p. 25; *The Wall Street Journal,* December 19, 1977.

# Appendix A

## Canadian Oil and Gas Resource Position

**Table A-1. Liquid Hydrocarbon Reserves in Canada—Original in Place, Ultimate and Remaining at December 31, 1976 (Thousand Barrels)**

| Provinces | Original in Place | | Ultimate Reserves | | Remaining Reserves | |
|---|---|---|---|---|---|---|
| | *Proved* | *Probable[a]* | *Proved* | *Probable[a]* | *Proved* | *Probable[a]* |
| Crude Oil | | | | | | |
| Territories | 500,000 | 500,000 | 60,000 | 90,000 | 38,717 | 68,717 |
| British Columbia | 1,283,648 | 1,293,848 | 412,525 | 439,056 | 135,294 | 161,825 |
| Alberta | 34,547,779 | 35,216,330 | 11,333,727 | 12,311,506 | 5,390,985 | 6,368,764 |
| Saskatchewan | 10,258,613 | 10,575,710 | 2,125,513 | 2,253,513 | 645,319 | 773,319 |
| Manitoba | 670,634 | 677,854 | 150,867 | 159,207 | 36,553 | 44,893 |
| Ontario | 197,149 | 203,876 | 64,218 | 66,409 | 10,143 | 12,334 |
| Other Eastern Canada | 18,000 | 18,000 | 850 | 2,324 | 71 | 1,545 |
| Total Canada | 47,475,823 | 48,485,618 | 14,147,700 | 15,322,015 | 6,257,082 | 7,431,397 |
| Natural Gas Liquids | | | | | | |
| Territories | | | 34,616 | 53,544 | 34,616 | 53,544 |
| British Columbia | | | 71,649 | 72,145 | 41,139 | 41,635 |
| Alberta[b] | | | 2,519,994 | 2,680,179 | 1,462,606 | 1,622,791 |
| Saskatchewan | | | 30,935 | 32,665 | 7,744 | 9,474 |
| Total Canada | | | 2,657,194 | 2,838,533 | 1,546,105 | 1,727,444 |

[a] Includes proved reserves.
[b] Including straddle plant recovery of NGL.

Source: American Petroleum Institute et al., *Reserves of Crude Oil, Natural Gas Liquids and Natural Gas in the United States and Canada, as of December 31, 1976*, Volume 31 (May 1977), p. 236.

**Table A-2. Changes in Liquid Hydrocarbon Reserves in Canada in 1976 (Thousand Barrels)**

| Provinces | Remaining Reserves at Dec. 31, 1975 (1) | 1976 Gross Additions Revisions (2) | Extensions (3) |
|---|---|---|---|
| Proved Reserves | | | |
| Crude Oil | | | |
| Territories | 39,796 | −75 | — |
| British Columbia | 146,487 | 3,292 | 279 |
| Alberta | 5,748,923 | −20,735 | 28,015 |
| Saskatchewan | 671,697 | 23,560 | 1,935 |
| Manitoba | 36,508 | 3,816 | 160 |
| Ontario | 9,515 | 1,267 | — |
| Other Eastern Canada | 76 | — | — |
| Total Crude Oil | 6,653,002 | 11,125 | 30,389 |
| Natural Gas Liquids | | | |
| Territories | 22,856 | 2,400 | 8,536 |
| British Columbia | 35,683 | 7,220 | 73 |
| Alberta[c] | 1,519,363 | 25,332 | 20,885 |
| Saskatchewan | 8,152 | 656 | — |
| Total Natural Gas Liquids | 1,586,054 | 35,608 | 29,494 |
| Total Liquid Hydrocarbons | 8,239,056 | 46,733 | 59,883 |
| Probable Reserves[b] | | | |
| Crude Oil | | | |
| Territories | 69,796 | | |
| British Columbia | 172,763 | | |
| Alberta | 6,725,220 | | |
| Saskatchewan | 805,426 | | |
| Manitoba | 46,048 | | |
| Ontario | 11,848 | | |
| Other Eastern Canada | 1,550 | | |
| Total Crude Oil | 7,832,651 | | |
| Natural Gas Liquids | | | |
| Territories | 41,112 | | |
| British Columbia | 36,703 | | |
| Alberta[c] | 1,664,120 | | |
| Saskatchewan | 9,967 | | |
| Total Natural Gas Liquids | 1,751,902 | | |
| Total Liquid Hydrocarbons | 9,584,553 | | |

[a] Preliminary estimate.
[b] Includes proved reserves.
[c] Including straddle plant recovery of NGL.
Note: Mackenzie Delta natural gas liquids reserves included for the first time in 1974.

Source: American Petroleum Institute *et al., Reserves of Crude Oil, Natural Gas Liquids and Natural Gas in the United States and Canada, as of December 31, 1976,* Volume 31 (May 1977), p. 228.

**Table A-2. Changes in Liquid Hydrocarbon Reserves in Canada in 1976 (Thousand Barrels) (continued)**

| 1976 Gross Additions | | 1976 Net Production[a] | Remaining Reserves at Dec. 31, 1976 | Net Change in Reserves during 1976 |
|---|---|---|---|---|
| *Discoveries* (4) | *Total* (5) | (6) | (7) | (8) |
| – | −75 | 1,004 | 38,717 | −1,079 |
| 60 | 3,631 | 14,824 | 135,294 | −11,193 |
| 910 | 8,190 | 366,128 | 5,390,985 | −357,938 |
| 105 | 25,600 | 51,978 | 645,319 | −26,378 |
| – | 3,976 | 3,931 | 36,553 | 45 |
| – | 1,267 | 639 | 10,143 | 628 |
| – | – | 5 | 71 | −5 |
| 1,075 | 42,589 | 438,509 | 6,257,082 | −395,920 |
| | | | | |
| 824 | 11,760 | – | 34,616 | 11,760 |
| – | 7,293 | 1,837 | 41,139 | 5,456 |
| 83 | 46,300 | 103,057 | 1,462,606 | −56,757 |
| – | 656 | 1,064 | 7,744 | −408 |
| 907 | 66,009 | 105,958 | 1,546,105 | −39,949 |
| 1,982 | 108,598 | 544,467 | 7,803,187 | −435,869 |
| | | | | |
| | −75 | 1,004 | 68,717 | −1,079 |
| | 3,886 | 14,824 | 161,825 | −10,938 |
| | 9,672 | 366,128 | 6,368,764 | −356,456 |
| | 19,871 | 51,978 | 773,319 | −32,107 |
| | 2,776 | 3,931 | 44,893 | −1,155 |
| | 1,125 | 639 | 12,334 | 486 |
| | – | 5 | 1,545 | −5 |
| | 37,255 | 438,509 | 7,431,397 | −401,254 |
| | | | | |
| | 12,432 | – | 53,544 | 12,432 |
| | 6,769 | 1,837 | 41,635 | 4,932 |
| | 61,728 | 103,057 | 1,622,791 | −41,329 |
| | 571 | 1,064 | 9,474 | −493 |
| | 81,500 | 105,958 | 1,727,444 | −24,458 |
| | 118,755 | 544,467 | 9,158,841 | −425,712 |

Figure A-1. Canada's Petroleum Basins

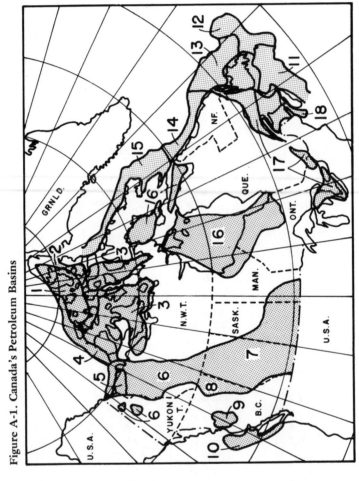

Source: Ministry of Energy, Mines and Resources, *An Energy Policy for Canada,*
Phase 1, Volume I–Analysis (1973), p. 85.

**Figure A-1. Canada's Petroleum Basins—Legend**

1. Sverdrup Basin
2. Arctic Fold Belt
3. Arctic Stable Platform
4. Arctic Coastal Plain (North)
5. Beaufort-Mackenzie
6. Mainland N.W.T.
7. Alta., Sask., Man.
8. N.E. British Columbia
9. Bowser Basin
10. West Coast Offshore
11. Scotian Basin (incl. Sydney Basin)
12. Avalon Uplift & Flemish Cap
13. East Newfoundland Basin
14. Labrador Shelf & Slope
15. Baffin Island Shelf & Slope
16. Hudson Platform
17. St. Lawrence Platform
18. Maritime Basins

**Table A-3. Natural Gas Reserves in Canada, Original in Place and Ultimate at December 31, 1976 (Million Cubic Feet at 14.65 psia and 60° F)**

| Provinces | Original Raw Gas in Place | | Ultimate Raw Gas Reserves | | Ultimate Marketable Gas Reserves | |
|---|---|---|---|---|---|---|
| | Proved | Probable[a] | Proved | Probable[a] | Proved | Probable[a] |
| Territories | 7,121,174 | 24,136,048 | 5,385,880 | 18,567,600 | 4,946,998 | 16,945,540 |
| British Columbia | 15,980,758 | 16,685,813 | 12,789,900 | 13,356,207 | 10,629,809 | 11,091,648 |
| Alberta | 116,927,796 | 124,708,157 | 86,004,944 | 92,278,484 | 68,509,889[b] | 73,833,950[b] |
| Saskatchewan | 4,257,954 | 4,732,298 | 2,357,050 | 2,704,536 | 1,694,321 | 1,981,839 |
| Manitoba | 58,441 | 59,128 | 13,209 | 14,025 | — | — |
| Ontario | 1,002,609 | 1,009,293 | 956,193 | 962,567 | 928,342 | 934,531 |
| Other Eastern Canada | 33,620 | 33,620 | 32,145 | 32,145 | 30,200 | 30,200 |
| Total Canada | 145,382,352 | 171,364,357 | 107,539,321 | 127,915,564 | 86,739,559 | 104,817,708 |

a Includes proved reserves.
b After adjustment for straddle plant processing shrinkage and fuel.
Source: American Petroleum Institute et al., *Reserves of Crude Oil, Natural Gas Liquids and Natural Gas in the United States and Canada, as of December 31, 1976*, Volume 31 (May 1977). p. 238.

**Table A-4. Changes in Marketable Natural Gas Reserves in Canada in 1976 (Million Cubic Feet at 14.65 psia and 60° F)**

| Provinces | Remaining Reserves at Dec. 31, 1975 (1) | Revisions (2) | 1976 Gross Additions | | Total (5) | Net Change in Underground Storage (6) | 1976 Net Production[a] (7) |
|---|---|---|---|---|---|---|---|
| | | | Extensions (3) | Discoveries (4) | | | |
| **Proved Reserves** | | | | | | | |
| Territories | 3,646,680 | 37,302 | 1,067,000 | 103,000 | 1,207,302 | — | 28,864 |
| British Columbia | 6,839,724 | – 42,181 | 155,112 | 37,977 | 150,908 | — | 298,589 |
| Alberta[c] | 45,324,508 | –398,868 | 2,363,878 | 487,947 | 2,452,957 | 503 | 2,153,804 |
| Saskatchewan | 897,353 | 2,554 | 2,000 | — | 4,554 | 217 | 55,292 |
| Ontario | 265,407 | 32,709 | — | 10,241 | 43,130 | –11,773 | 4,528 |
| Other Eastern Canada | 1,044 | 604 | | | 604 | — | 99 |
| Total Canada | 56,974,716 | –367,880 | 3,587,990 | 639,345 | 3,859,455 | –11,053 | 2,541,176 |
| **Probable Reserves[b]** | | | | | | | |
| Territories | 11,667,222 | | | | 5,185,302 | — | 28,864 |
| British Columbia | 7,425,500 | | | | 26,971 | — | 298,589 |
| Alberta[c] | 50,924,027 | | | | 2,177,240 | 503 | 2,153,804 |
| Saskatchewan | 1,179,287 | | | | 10,138 | 217 | 55,292 |
| Ontario | 269,666 | | | | 45,060 | –11,773 | 4,528 |
| Other Eastern Canada | 1,071 | | | | 577 | — | 99 |
| Total Canada | 71,466,773 | | | | 7,445,288 | –11,053 | 2,541,176 |

Source: American Petroleum Institute et al., *Reserves of Crude Oil, Natural Gas Liquids and Natural Gas in the United States and Canada, as of December 31, 1976*, Volume 31 (May 1977), p. 229.

(Table continued on p. 82)

**Table A-4. Changes in Marketable Natural Gas Reserves in Canada in 1976 (Million Cubic Feet at 14.65 psia and 60° F) (continued)**

| Provinces | Non-Associated (8) | Associated (9) | 1976 Gross Additions | | Total (12) | Net Change in Reserves during 1976 (13) |
| --- | --- | --- | --- | --- | --- | --- |
| | | | Dissolved (10) | Underground Storage (11) | | |
| **Proved Reserves** | | | | | | |
| Territories | 4,825,118 | – | – | – | 4,825,118 | 1,178,438 |
| British Columbia | 6,295,102 | 322,811 | 74,130 | – | 6,692,043 | –147,681 |
| Alberta[c] | 37,797,330 | 5,877,666 | 1,928,357 | 20,811 | 45,624,164 | 299,656 |
| Saskatchewan | 740,809 | 42,234 | 53,392 | 10,397 | 846,832 | –50,521 |
| Ontario | 123,788 | – | – | 168,448 | 292,236 | 26,829 |
| Other Eastern Canada | 31 | 1,518 | – | – | 1,549 | 505 |
| Total Canada | 49,782,178 | 6,244,229 | 2,055,879 | 199,656 | 58,281,942 | 1,307,226 |
| **Probable Reserves[b]** | | | | | | |
| Territories | 16,823,660 | – | – | – | 16,823,660 | 5,156,438 |
| British Columbia | 6,740,034 | 337,218 | 76,630 | – | 7,153,882 | –271,618 |
| Alberta[c] | 42,588,988 | 6,026,926 | 2,311,241 | 20,811 | 50,947,966 | 23,939 |
| Saskatchewan | 1,017,274 | 45,383 | 61,296 | 10,397 | 1,134,350 | –44,937 |
| Ontario | 129,977 | – | – | 168,448 | 298,425 | 28,759 |
| Other Eastern Canada | 31 | 1,518 | – | – | 1,549 | 478 |
| Total Canada | 67,299,964 | 6,411,045 | 2,449,167 | 199,656 | 76,359,832 | 4,893,059 |

[a] Preliminary estimate.
[b] Includes proved reserves.
[c] After adjustment for straddle plant processing shrinkage and fuel.
Note: Mackenzie Delta gas reserves included for the first time in 1974. Arctic Islands gas reserves included for the first time in 1975.

# Appendix B

## Canadian Energy Supply and Demand Projections

**Table B-1. Canadian Requirements for Crude Oil and Equivalent
1977 NEB Forecast[a]
(Million barrels/day)**

|  | *1976* | *1980* | *1985* | *1990* | *1995* |
|---|---|---|---|---|---|
| Product Sales | 1,658 | 1,922 | 2,099 | 2,231 | 2,431 |
| West of Ottawa Valley | 899 | 1,056 | 1,146 | 1,244 | 1,358 |
| East of Ottawa Valley | 759 | 866 | 953 | 987 | 1,073 |
| Adjustments[b] | 33 | 95 | 97 | 46 | 53 |
| West of Ottawa Valley | − 14 | 117 | 94 | 41 | 47 |
| East of Ottawa Valley | 47 | − 22 | 3 | 5 | 6 |
| Imported Feedstocks | 716 | 594 | 706 | 742 | 829 |
| West of Ottawa Valley | − | − | − | − | − |
| East of Ottawa Valley | 716 | 594 | 706 | 742 | 829 |
| Canadian Feedstocks | 975 | 1,423 | 1,490 | 1,535 | 1,655 |
| West of Ottawa Valley | 885 | 1,173 | 1,240 | 1,285 | 1,405 |
| East of Ottawa Valley | 90 | 250 | 250 | 250 | 250 |

[a] Medium case (See Note b, Table B-2).
[b] Includes net product imports, losses, industry use, and others.
Source: National Energy Board, *Canadian Oil Supply & Requirements*
(February 1977), Appendix L.

Figure B.1. Canadian Supply and Requirements of Crude Oil and Equivalent Range of NEB Scenarios

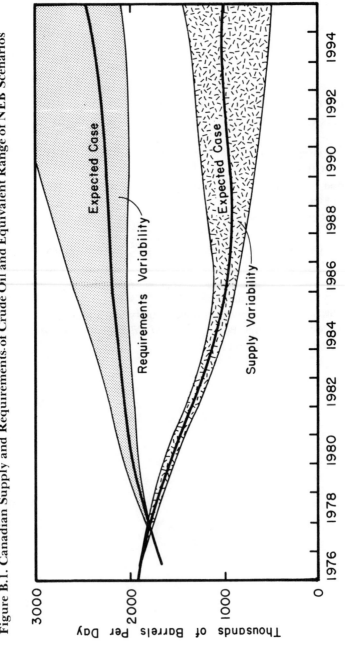

Source: National Energy Board, *Canadian Oil Supply & Requirements* (February 1977), p. 85.

**Table B-2. Canadian Refined Petroleum Product Demand
West of Ottawa Valley –Alternative Scenarios for 1976-1995
(Million barrels/day)**

|                          | 1976  | 1980    | 1985    | 1990    | 1995    |
|--------------------------|-------|---------|---------|---------|---------|
| Minimum Case[a]          | 896.1 | 1,025.9 | 1,071.6 | 1,111.5 | 1,169.4 |
| Medium Case[b]           | 899.1 | 1,056.4 | 1,145.7 | 1,243.8 | 1,357.9 |
| Maximum Case[c]          | 904.0 | 1,112.3 | 1,353.7 | 1,649.2 | 1,965.7 |

[a] Assumes medium economic growth and international crude oil prices rising in real terms at 5% per annum after 1975.
[b] Assumes medium economic growth and international crude oil prices constant in real terms at 1975 level.
[c] Assumes high economic growth and international oil prices constant in nominal terms after 1975.
Source: National Energy Board, *Canadian Oil Supply & Requirements* (February 1977), Tables VIII-4 and VIII-6.

**Table B-3. Potential Producibility of Canadian Crude Oil
and Equivalent NEB Forecast
(Million barrels/day)**

|                       | 1976  | 1980  | 1985  | 1990 | 1995  |
|-----------------------|-------|-------|-------|------|-------|
| Expected Case         |       |       |       |      |       |
| Established Reserves   | 1,716 | 1,194 | 628   | 352  | 209   |
| Reserves Additions     | –     | 63    | 137   | 189  | 204   |
| Pentanes Plus          | 145   | 120   | 87    | 63   | 44    |
| Oil Sands              | 55    | 156   | 205   | 355  | 575   |
| Total                 | 1,916 | 1,533 | 1,057 | 959  | 1,032 |
| Possible Range[a]     |       |       |       |      |       |
| Minimum Case           |       | 1,500 | 970   | 685  | 525   |
| Maximum Case           |       | 1,565 | 1,140 | 1,260| 1,420 |

[a] Includes estimates for reserve additions.
Source: National Energy Board, *Canadian Oil Supply & Requirements*, (February 1977), Figures II-7 and II-8, Appendices D, E and F.

Figure B-2. Canadian Gas Supply-Demand Balance for Conventional Producing Areas

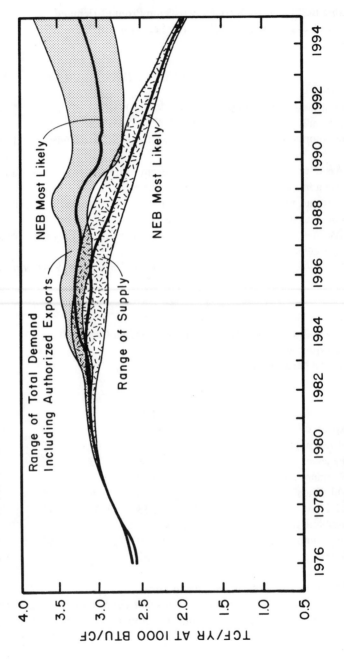

Source: National Energy Board, *Reasons for Decision Northern Pipelines*, Volume 1 (June 1977), Figure 2-10.

**Table B-4. Total Demand for Canadian Natural Gas for 1977-1995
(Bcf/year @ 1,000 BTU/cf)**

|  | *1977* | *1980* | *1985* | *1990* | *1995* |
|---|---|---|---|---|---|
| Alberta | 400 | 537 | 649 | 731 | 819 |
| British Columbia | 169 | 194 | 241 | 267 | 317 |
| East of Alberta | 1,025 | 1,179 | 1,393 | 1,652 | 1,922 |
| Net Reprocessing | 101 | 164 | 153 | 132 | 128 |
| Domestic Demand | 1,695 | 2,073 | 2,436 | 2,781 | 3,186 |
| Exports[a] | 1,045 | 999 | 896 | 215 | 6 |
| Total Demand | 2,740 | 3,072 | 3,332 | 2,996 | 3,192 |

[a] Export requirements adjusted to reflect make-up provisions in the license.

Source: National Energy Board, *Reasons for Decision Northern Pipelines,* Volume 1 (June 1977), Appendix 2-3.

**Table B-5. Potential Canadian Gas Deliverability for 1977-1995
(Bcf/year @ 1,000 BTU/cf)**

|  | *1977* | *1980* | *1985* | *1990* | *1995* |
|---|---|---|---|---|---|
| Established Areas | | | | | |
| Total Committed | | | | | |
| Reserves | 2,627 | 2,763 | 2,213 | 1,419 | 821 |
| Alberta Uncommitted | 47 | 222 | 278 | 240 | 157 |
| Alberta Deferred | – | – | 28 | 28 | 23 |
| Trend Supply[a] | 1 | 84 | 630 | 964 | 950 |
| Total | 2,675 | 3,069 | 3,149 | 2,651 | 1,951 |
| Frontier Areas[b] | – | – | 255 | 255 | 255 |
| Total Deliverability | 2,675 | 3,069 | 3,404 | 2,906 | 2,206 |

[a] Supply from estimated future discoveries.
[b] NEB forecast for Mackenzie Delta-Beaufort Sea only. Deliverability of natural gas assumed to begin in 1985.

Source: National Energy Board, *Reasons for Decision Northern Pipelines,* Volume 1 (June 1977), Appendix 2-3 and pp. 2-140.

**Table B-6. Canadian Coal Demand and Supply for 1975-1990**

**A. Possible Coal Demand**

| Economic Growth | High-Price Scenario | | Low-Price Scenario | |
|---|---|---|---|---|
| | High | Low | High | Low |
| | *(millions of tons)* | | | |
| 1975* | 28.0 | 28.0 | 28.0 | 28.0 |
| 1980 | 39.8 | 39.8 | 40.8 | 40.8 |
| 1985 | 50.3 | 48.7 | 53.5 | 51.8 |
| 1990 | 66.0 | 58.9 | 70.7 | 63.4 |
| | *Average Annual Growth Rates (%)* | | | |
| 1976-80 | 7.3 | 7.3 | 7.8 | 7.8 |
| 1981-90 | 5.2 | 4.0 | 5.7 | 4.5 |
| 1976-90 | 5.9 | 5.1 | 6.4 | 5.6 |

**B. Possible Coal Supply**
**(millions of tons)**

| | *1975** | *1980* | *1985* | *1990* |
|---|---|---|---|---|
| Low rank thermal | 10.4 | 19.4 | 39.9 | 74.3 |
| High rank thermal | 2.3 | 4.2 | 6.0 | 7.2 |
| Metallurgical | 15.0 | 21.3 | 34.6 | 36.6 |
| Total | 27.7 | 44.9 | 80.5 | 118.1 |

*Estimate.
Source: Ministry of Energy, Mines and Resources, *An Energy Strategy for Canada* (1976), Tables 7 and 11.

**Table B-7. Canadian Electricity Demand and Capacity for 1975-1990**

**A. Possible Electricity Demand**

| Economic Growth | High-Price Scenario | | Low-Price Scenario | |
|---|---|---|---|---|
| | *High* | *Low* | *High* | *Low* |
| | *(billions of kilowatt-hours)* | | | |
| 1975[a] | 266 | 266 | 266 | 266 |
| 1980 | 355 | 355 | 369 | 369 |
| 1985 | 450 | 435 | 486 | 471 |
| 1990 | 592 | 538 | 642 | 586 |
| | *Average Annual Growth Rates (%)* | | | |
| 1976-80 | 5.9 | 5.9 | 6.8 | 6.8 |
| 1981-90 | 5.2 | 4.2 | 5.7 | 4.7 |
| 1976-90 | 5.5 | 4.8 | 6.0 | 5.4 |

[a] Estimate.

(Table continued on p. 92.)

**Table B-7. Canadian Electricity Demand and Capacity for 1975-1990 (continued)**

**B. Projections of Installed Electrical Capacity (Megawatts)**

|  | *Hydro* | *High-Growth Case* | | *Total* |
|---|---|---|---|---|
|  |  | *Nuclear* | *Other[b]* |  |
| 1975[a] | 36,800 | 2,660 | 20,080 | 59,540 |
| 1980 | 46,700 | 6,900 | 25,400 | 79,100 |
| 1985 | 61,900 | 17,800 | 31,400 | 111,100 |
| 1990 | 72,500 | 29,500 | 49,800 | 151,800 |

|  | *Hydro* | *Low-Growth Case* | | *Total* |
|---|---|---|---|---|
|  |  | *Nuclear* | *Other[b]* |  |
| 1975[a] | 36,800 | 2,660 | 20,080 | 59,540 |
| 1980 | 42,500 | 6,200 | 23,700 | 72,400 |
| 1985 | 55,500 | 12,800 | 29,500 | 97,800 |
| 1990 | 66,200 | 22,200 | 36,800 | 125,200 |

Note: The high-growth case reflects the expansion plans of provincial utilities as of end-1975. The recent announcements of delays in capacity expansion programs are not reflected. The low-growth case has been generated within Energy, Mines and Resources and represents a capacity expansion program to meet load growths that increase on average by 5.5% per year from 1976-1990.

[a] Estimate.

[b] Other generation includes electrical power generated from coal, oil and natural gas.

Source: Ministry of Energy, Mines and Resources, *An Energy Strategy for Canada* (1976), Tables 6 and 10.

# Appendix C
## Canada-U.S. Energy Trade

**Table C-1. U.S. Pipeline Imports and Exports of Natural Gas[a], 1955-1976 (MMcf)**

| Year | Imports from Canada | Imports from Mexico | Total Imports |
|------|------|------|------|
| 1955 | 10,885 | 7 | 10,892 |
| 1956 | 10,586 | 6 | 10,592 |
| 1957 | 21,060 | 16,970 | 38,030 |
| 1958 | 88,230 | 46,211 | 134,441 |
| 1959 | 81,892 | 50,929 | 132,821 |
| 1960 | 109,855 | 46,988 | 156,843 |
| 1961 | 168,822 | 51,755 | 220,577 |
| 1962 | 342,770 | 51,066 | 393,836 |
| 1963 | 357,961 | 49,762 | 407,723 |
| 1964 | 392,239 | 52,620 | 444,859 |
| 1965 | 404,687 | 52,007 | 456,694 |
| 1966 | 431,955 | 48,636 | 480,491 |
| 1967 | 513,256 | 50,972 | 564,228 |
| 1968 | 604,462 | 47,423 | 651,885 |
| 1969 | 680,107 | 46,845 | 726,952 |
| 1970 | 778,688 | 41,336 | 820,024 |
| 1971 | 910,925 | 20,689 | 931,615 |
| 1972 | 1,009,092 | 8,140 | 1,017,233 |
| 1973 | 1,027,216 | 1,632 | 1,028,848 |
| 1974 | 959,063 | 222 | 959,285 |
| 1975 | 948,115 | 0 | 948,115 |
| 1976 | 953,613 | 0 | 953,613 |

[a] Volumes reported for 1966 and later are @ 14.73 Psia and 60° F. Volumes for 1965 and prior are "as reported." LNG imports and exports are excluded.

Source: Federal Power Commission, "United States Imports and Exports of Natural Gas, 1976" (May 1977), p. 4.

(Table continued on p. 96.)

**Table C-1. U.S. Pipeline Imports and Exports of Natural Gas[a], 1955-1976 (MMcf) (continued)**

| *Exports to Canada* | *Exports to Mexico* | *Total Exports* | *Net Imports* |
|---|---|---|---|
| 11,494 | 19,903 | 31,397 | (20,505) |
| 17,499 | 19,499 | 36,663 | (26,071) |
| 25,368 | 14,998 | 40,366 | ( 2,336) |
| 32,128 | 10,790 | 42,918 | 91,523 |
| 11,740 | 10,794 | 22,534 | 110,287 |
| 5,574 | 10,526 | 16,100 | 140,743 |
| 5,578 | 9,638 | 15,216 | 205,361 |
| 5,575 | 10,255 | 15,830 | 378,006 |
| 6,880 | 10,068 | 16,948 | 390,775 |
| 9,654 | 9,842 | 19,496 | 425,363 |
| 17,892 | 9,536 | 27,428 | 429,266 |
| 44,958 | 9,902 | 54,860 | 425,631 |
| 70,456 | 11,139 | 81,595 | 482,633 |
| 81,647 | 12,098 | 93,745 | 558,140 |
| 34,936 | 13,390 | 48,326 | 678,626 |
| 10,860 | 14,678 | 25,538 | 794,486 |
| 14,349 | 15,785 | 30,134 | 901,481 |
| 15,553 | 14,579 | 30,132 | 987,101 |
| 14,824 | 13,999 | 28,823 | 1,000,025 |
| 13,263 | 13,268 | 26,531 | 932,754 |
| 10,219 | 9,454 | 19,673 | 928,442 |
| 7,506 | 7,425 | 14,931 | 938,682 |

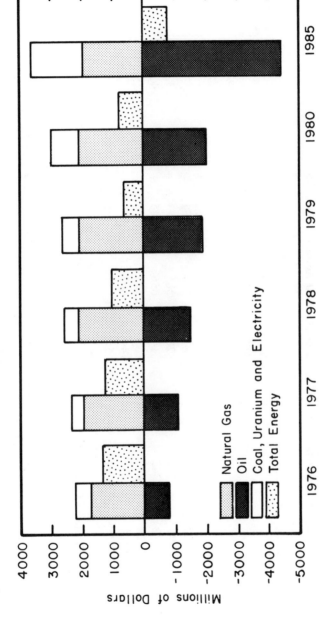

Figure C-1. Projected Canadian Balance of Trade in Energy Commodities

Source: Ministry of Energy, Mines and Resources, *An Energy Strategy for Canada* (1976), p. 113.

**Table C-2. Canadian Balance of Payments, Current Account 1970-1975**

*Balance of Trade[a] in*

| | Oil | Natural Gas | Other Energy Commodities | Total Energy Commodities | Total Merchandise including Energy[b] | Services[b] | Current Account[b] |
|---|---|---|---|---|---|---|---|
| 1970 | 128 | 201 | − 82 | 247 | 3,052 | −2,099 | 953 |
| 1971 | 170 | 244 | − 28 | 385 | 2,427 | −2,395 | 32 |
| 1972 | 343 | 299 | 14 | 656 | 1,645 | −2,590 | − 945 |
| 1973 | 647 | 343 | 162 | 1,152 | 2,720 | −3,039 | − 319 |
| 1974 | 1,036 | 488 | 144 | 1,668 | 1,519 | −3,706 | −2,187 |
| 1975[c] | 91 | 1,085 | 55 | 1,231 | − 795 | −4,690 | −5,485 |

[a] Trade of Canada basis.
[b] National Accounts basis.
[c] Preliminary.
Source: Ministry of Energy, Mines and Resources, *An Energy Strategy for Canada* (1976), p. 113.

**Figure C-2. U.S.-Canadian Oil[a] Trade**

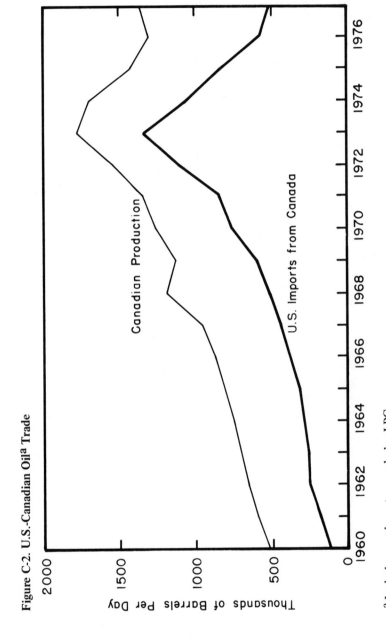

[a] Includes condensates, excludes LPGs.

Sources: U.S. Bureau of Mines, *Energy Perspectives*, 2 (June 1976); *The Oil and Gas Journal*, Worldwide reports for 1976 and 1977.

**Table C-3. U.S. Imports of Canadian Oil, 1960-1977**
**(Million barrels/day)**

| Year | Crude Petroleum | Petroleum Products | Total[a] |
|------|-----------------|--------------------|---------|
| 1960 | 113 | 9 | 122 |
| 1961 | 183 | 10 | 193 |
| 1962 | 233 | 17 | 250 |
| 1963 | 248 | 17 | 265 |
| 1964 | 278 | 21 | 299 |
| 1965 | 295 | 28 | 323 |
| 1966 | 347 | 37 | 384 |
| 1967 | 412 | 38 | 450 |
| 1968 | 464 | 44 | 508 |
| 1969 | 557 | 51 | 608 |
| 1970 | 672 | 94 | 766 |
| 1971 | 721 | 136 | 857 |
| 1972 | 856 | 255 | 1,111 |
| 1973 | 1,001 | 324 | 1,325 |
| 1974 | 791 | 277 | 1,068 |
| 1975 | 600 | 246 | 846 |
| 1976 | 371 | 228 | 599 |
| 1977[a] | 279 | 238 | 517 |

[a] January through June.
Source: U.S. Department of the Interior, *Energy Perspectives 2* (June 1976), pp. 191-195 for 1960-1974; "Petroleum Statement Annual," Table 25 for 1975-76; 1977 by telephone.

**Figure C-3. Canadian Share of U.S. Energy Market**

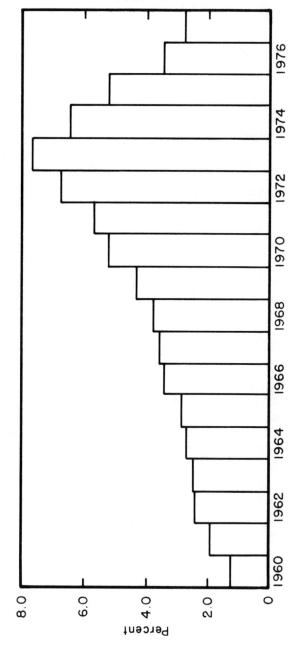

Sources: U.S. Bureau of Mines, *Energy Perspectives*, 2 (June 1976); *The Oil and Gas Journal*, Worldwide reports for 1976 and 1977.

**Table C-4. U.S. Imports of Canadian Petroleum as a Percentage of Total U.S. Petroleum Demand, 1960-1977**

| Years | Market Percentage |
|-------|-------------------|
| 1960 | 1.24 |
| 1961 | 1.93 |
| 1962 | 2.41 |
| 1963 | 2.47 |
| 1964 | 2.71 |
| 1965 | 2.81 |
| 1966 | 3.41 |
| 1967 | 3.58 |
| 1968 | 3.78 |
| 1969 | 4.30 |
| 1970 | 5.21 |
| 1971 | 5.63 |
| 1972 | 6.77 |
| 1973 | 7.66 |
| 1974 | 6.41 |
| 1975 | 5.18 |
| 1976 | 3.43 |
| 1977[a] | 2.77 |

[a] January through June rate.

Source: U.S. Department of the Interior, *Energy Perspectives 2* (June 1976, pp. 63 and 191-195 for 1960-1974; Petroleum Industry Research Foundation, Inc., *U.S. Oil Imports by Type of Oil and Area of Origin, Annual 1974-1976,* March 1977, Tables IV and VIII for 1975-1976.

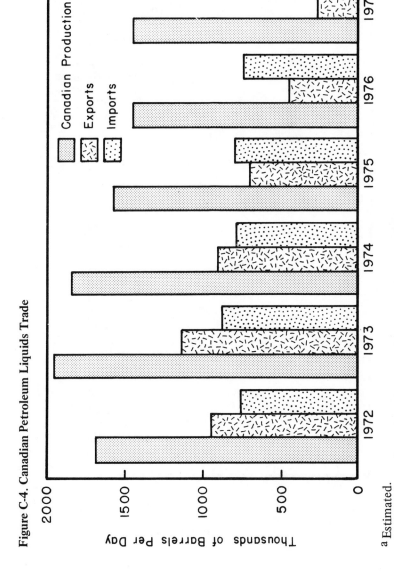

Figure C-4. Canadian Petroleum Liquids Trade

a Estimated.
Source: National Energy Board, *Annual Report 76*, p. 15 and 77, p. 20.

Figure C-5. Dollar Value of Canadian Exports of Oil, Gas and Electricity

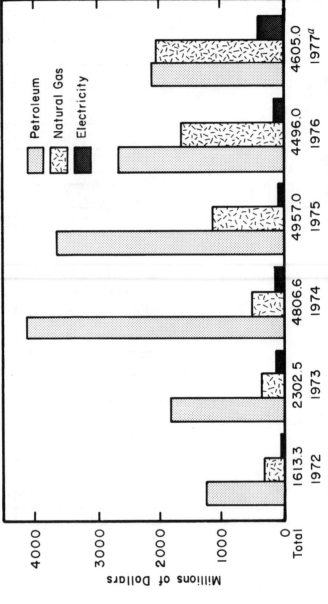

a Estimated.

Source: National Energy Board, *Annual Report 76*, p. 26 and 77, p. 32.

**Figure C-6. Major Oil and Gas Pipelines in Canada**

Source: Canadian Imperial Bank of Commerce, based on data provided by the Alberta Petroleum and Natural Gas Department.

**Figure C-7. Alcan Pipeline Project**

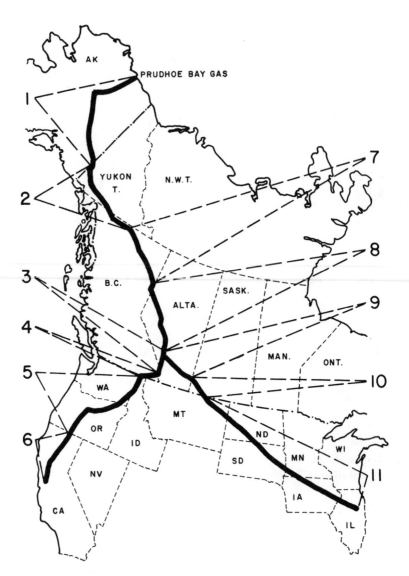

Source: Federal Power Commission, *Recommendation to the President, Alaska Natural Gas Transportation Systems,* May 1, 1977, p. II-17.

**Figure C-7. Alcan Pipeline Project—Legend**

1. Alcan Pipeline Company, 731 miles, 48 inch line
2. Foothills Pipe Lines (Yukon) Ltd., 513 miles, 48 inch line
3. Alberta Gas Trunk Line (Canada) Ltd., 176 miles, 36 inch line
4. Westcoast Transmission Company, Ltd., 105 miles, 36 inch line
5. Pacific Gas Transmission Company, 592 miles, 36 inch looping
6. Pacific Gas & Electric Company, 282 miles, 36 inch looping
7. Westcoast Transmission Company Ltd., 438 miles, 48 inch line
8. Alberta Gas Trunk Line (Canada) Ltd., 395 miles, 48 inch line
9. Alberta Gas Trunk Line (Canada) Ltd., 235 miles, 42 inch line
10. Foothills Pipe Lines (Yukon) Ltd., 160 miles, 42 inch line
11. Northern Border Pipeline Company, 1,117 miles, 42 inch line

**Figure C-8. Canadian International and Interprovincial Transfers of Electricity for 1976**

Source: National Energy Board, *Annual Report, 1977,* p. 30.

# Appendix D
## Canadian Crude Oil Export Formula, October 1974

**Protection for Canadian Requirements**

In determining the allowable level of crude oil and equivalent exports for 1977 the Board will employ the formula outlined in its October 1974 and September 1975 reports. However, in contrast to previous years, the procedure will be applied separately for heavy crude oil and light crude oil and equivalent. The procedure used to calculate allowable exports is expressed in the formula as follows:

$$E = [P - (D+C)] \frac{t}{10}$$

Where E is the average annual volume in mb/d available for export licensing during the year for which the determination is made.

Where P is the forecast annual average potential producibility of crude oil and equivalent in mb/d during the year for which the determination is made.

Where D is the forecast annual average requirements for Canadian use in mb/d of indigenous crude oil and equivalent during the year for which the determination is made.

Where C is the forecast total increase that would have occurred in requirements for indigenous crude oil and equivalent in mb/d if conservation measures since 1972 had not been effective.

Where t is the time during which supply is forecast to exceed Canadian requirements, from 1 January of the year for which the determination is made, expressed to the nearest tenth of a year, and extended to a maximum of 10 years.

*Light Crude Oil and Equivalent*

Using parameters previously determined in this report and

Figure D-1. Calculation of Allowable Exports of Canadian Light Crude Oil and Equivalent

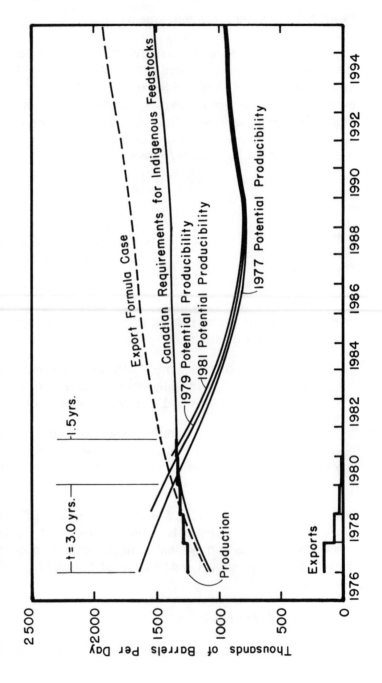

illustrated in Figure D-1, volumes of light crude oil and equivalent available for licensing in 1977 are:

$$E = [P - (D+C)] \frac{t}{10}$$

$$= [1616 - (1133+25)] \frac{3}{10}$$

$$= 137 \text{ Mb/d}$$

The calculation shown above can be repeated for subsequent years to show the effect the protection procedure might have on exports in the future and how long the supply-demand intersection can be delayed. For each year considered, a new potential producibility projection must be constructed to account for the carry-forward effect of production at rates lower than capacity. The effect of this carry-forward as illustrated in Figure D-2 ends with a 1981 potential producibility curve, which intersects the Canadian requirements curve in mid-1981, after which time Canadian production of light crude oil and equivalent will no longer be sufficient to meet WOV requirements plus shipments to Montreal.

Using this method, future allowable exports of light crude oil and equivalent are accordingly estimated to be:

| Year | Allowable Exports Mb/d |
|------|------------------------|
| 1978 | 54 |
| 1979 | 20 |
| 1980 | 1 |
| 1981 | 0 |

As light crude oil exports are reduced to zero, the Board expects that exceptions to its broad policy of phasing-out light crude oil and equivalent exports will likely be necessary. As mentioned in Chapter VI synthetic crude oil and condensate may become available in excess of the calculated surplus volume and operational constraints may also require future light crude oil and equivalent exports.

Figure D-2. Calculation of Allowable Exports of Canadian Heavy Crude Oil

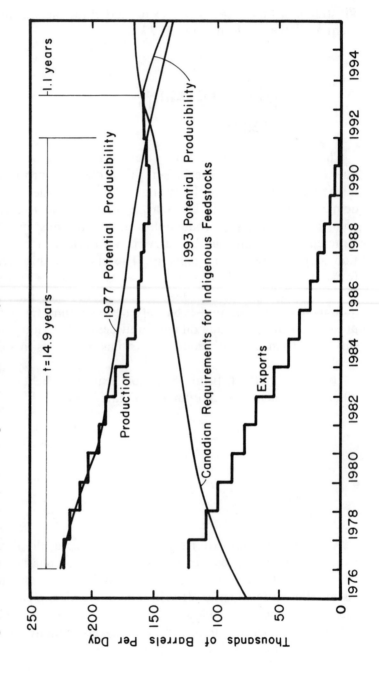

## Heavy Crude Oil

Similar parameters have been determined for heavy crude oil. These parameters are shown in Figure D-2. Allowable heavy crude oil exports for 1977 are calculated to be:

$$E = [P - (D+C)] \frac{t}{10}$$

$$= [221 - (98+0)] \times 1 \text{ because } t > 10 \text{ years}$$

$$= 123 \text{ Mb/d}$$

When t exceeds 10 years in the Board's export control procedures, the only restriction placed on exports is that feedstock requirements of Canadian refineries must be met first. The remainder of productive capacity is then available for export. Consequently the value 123 Mb/d should only be viewed as an estimate of the volume of heavy crude oil which will be available for export during 1977. The actual value will depend on actual monthly productive capacity and Canadian requirements.

As in the case for light crude oil and equivalent exports, the above calculation can be repeated for subsequent years to estimate. long term trends in heavy crude oil exports, as follows:

| Year | Allowable Exports Mb/d |
|------|------------------------|
| 1978 | 110[a] |
| 1979 | 99[a] |
| 1980 | 88[a] |
| 1981 | 77[a] |
| 1982 | 68 |
| 1983 | 54 |
| 1984 | 42 |
| 1985 | 32 |
| 1986 | 26 |

[a]Estimated to be greater than 10 years. Exports restricted only by productive capacity and Canadian requirements for heavy crude oil.

It should be noted that these calculations exclude the effect that a heavy crude oil upgrading facility would have on Canadian requirements for heavy crude oil feedstocks. The Board is aware that studies are now underway to fully evaluate the technical and economic feasibility of building plants to process heavy crude oil into synthetic light crude oil. In application of the export formula to the Board's estimates of supply and requirements for light and heavy crude oil the Board has not adjusted the estimates to account for the effects of upgrading heavy crude oil. Although there are several ways that upgrading could be accounted for in the separate application of the export formula the net effect of processing heavy crude oil into synthetic light crude oil would be to create additional Canadian requirements for heavy crude oil and additional supply of light crude oil and equivalent. Such a project would therefore "transfer" oil from the heavy crude oil category where there is sufficient supply to meet forecast Canadian requirements for 13 years to the light crude and equivalent category where "t" is only three years.

The Board considers the maximization of Canadian heavy crude oil use in Canada to be in the national interest primarily because in the future Canada will have to rely to a much greater degree on oil sands and heavy crude oil reserves. Upgrading heavy crude oil, whether in existing refineries or in new facilities, will have the effect of shifting Canada's energy reliance from steadily depleting light crude oil reservoirs to the greater potential heavy crude oil deposits.

At the present time the Board is unable to speculate as to the outcome of studies now underway. There is some likelihood that upgrading facilities will be constructed and given favorable conditions could perhaps be on stream in the early 1980s. It is the Board's view, however, that several areas of present uncertainty will have to be overcome before investment would proceed:

- federal and provincial taxation policies will have to be clear to investors; term commitments regarding taxation, royalties and prices may have to be made,

- experimental recovery methods will have to be confirmed; pilot studies now underway will require further time to prove effectiveness of enhanced recovery methods and well equipment design, and

- market availability and confidence will have to be evident for companies to develop heavy crude oil producibility in anticipation of assured markets through upgrading.

In response in part to these needs the Board has moved to separately license heavy crude oil and will further evaluate the feasibility of extending the term of heavy crude oil licenses.

Source: National Energy Board, *Canadian Oil Supply and Requirements,* February 1977, pp. 70-73.

# Appendix E

## Canada's Oil
## and Gas Industry: History

**Pre-1973**

| | |
|---|---|
| 1858 | North America's first producing oil well in Ontario. |
| 1914 | Turner Valley oil discovery. |
| 1947 | Leduc oil discovery. |
| 1950 | Interprovincial Pipe Lines oil shipment as far east as Superior, Wisconsin. |
| 1953 | Trans Mountain Oil Pipe Lines oil shipment to Vancouver. |
| 1954 | Direct oil shipments to Sarnia. |
| 1954 | Direct oil shipments to Puget Sound. |
| 1957 | Westcoast Transmission Co. Ltd. natural gas line to Vancouver completed. |
| 1958 | TransCanada PipeLines Ltd. natural gas line to Eastern Canada completed. |
| 1959 | National Energy Board established. |
| 1961 | National Oil Policy established. |
| 1965 | Marketable gas production reaches one trillion ($10^{12}$) cubic feet. |
| 1966 | Liquid hydrocarbon production reaches 1 million barrels per day. |
| 1969 | Arctic Islands gas discovery. |
| 1970 | Liquid hydrocarbon production equals domestic demand for the first time. |
| 1970 | Mackenzie Delta oil discovery. |
| 1970 | Canada for the first time denies full authorization for additional exports of natural gas for reasons of inadequate surplus. |
| 1972 | Exports of gas reach one trillion ($10^{12}$) cubic feet. |

**1973**

| | |
|---|---|
| *March* | — Crude oil export controls announced. |
| *June* | — Export controls instituted for most petroleum products. |
| | — "An Energy Policy for Canada—Phase 1" published. |

| | |
|---|---|
| *August* | — Policy on uranium enrichment announced. |
| *September* | — Price restraint program for crude oil and petroleum products initiated. |
| | — Government's intention of extending Interprovincial Pipeline to Montreal announced. |
| *October* | — Crude oil export charge established. |
| | — An energy supply contingency plan was established, in light of curtailed international production and selective embargoes. |
| *December* | — A bill to establish an Energy Supplies Allocation Board was introduced in the House of Commons. It was subsequently approved by Parliament in January of 1974. |
| | — The Prime Minister placed before the House of Commons a proposal to set the basis for a new national oil policy to include a national market for oil with a single price, the establishment of a national oil company, the extension of the oil pipeline to Montreal, and intensification of research on oil sands technology. |
| | — A bill to provide for the imposition of an export charge was introduced in the House of Commons and was approved in January of 1974. The charge rose from 40 cents in October of 1973 to $6.40 in February of 1974. |

**1974**

| | |
|---|---|
| *January* | — The federal government announced a policy of an all-Canadian coast-to-coast pipeline network to develop self-reliance in oil and details of the Interprovincial Pipeline extension to Montreal. |
| | — First Ministers' Conference on Energy held. In addition to discussing the matter of an oil price increase, the federal government announced programs of assistance to encourage the expansion of electrical production based on |

nuclear energy and the interconnection of provincial utilities to insure greater efficiency and security. A policy statement was also made concerning the protection of uranium reserves for the domestic market, further processing requirements, stockpile use, and on support for uranium exploration.

– The Oil Import Compensation Program became effective on January 1 to provide for a single crude oil price across Canada subject only to transportation and quality differences.

– Establishment of an Office of Energy Conservation within the Department of Energy, Mines and Resources, to develop and recommend a program of energy conservation and to play a coordinating role among all institutions and authorities who would have responsibilities in conservation efforts.

– Establishment of an Office of Energy R & D within the Department of Energy, Mines and Resources to review, assess and coordinate the activities of the federal government in Energy R & D.

*March*

– First Ministers' Conference reconvened and agreement was reached on a price increase to $6.50 a barrel from $3.80, effective April 1.

– Mr. Justice Thomas R. Berger was appointed by the Government of Canada to inquire into, and report upon, the terms and conditions for a right-of-way that may be granted for a natural gas pipeline to cross Crown Lands in the Northwest Territories and the Yukon.

*September*

– The federal government announced a decision, based on a report of the National Energy Board, to establish a border export price for natural gas of $1.00/Mcf, effective January 1, 1975.

– The Minister of Energy, Mines and Resources

issued a major uranium policy statement on September 5 setting out the terms under which uranium exports would be permitted having regard to future Canadian requirements and the adequacy of reserves to meet those requirements.

*November*   – Federal budget dealt with fiscal arrangements related to petroleum industry.

– The Minister of Energy, Mines and Resources announced the findings of the National Energy Board with respect to the exportation of oil and the federal government's decision to accept the board's findings that steps should be taken to reduce exports of oil with a view to providing additional protection for Canadian requirements.

– Throughout 1974 Canada participated in international preparations leading to an "Agreement on an International Energy Program" creating the International Energy Agency (IEA) under the auspices of the Organization for Economic Cooperation and Development. The agreement was signed in November 1974 and came into effect in January 1976.

*December*   – The Minister of Energy, Mines and Resources announced more stringent safeguards in respect of the sale abroad of Canadian nuclear technology, facilities and material.

**1975**

*February*   – The Governments of Canada, Alberta and Ontario reached an agreement with the three private participants of Syncrude Canada Limited to form a new partnership to continue to build and to operate the Syncrude plant.

– The Minister of Energy, Mines and Resources announced an energy conservation program for Canada.

— Another in a series of oil price guidelines was announced, to provide in this case provision for oil companies to recover non-crude cost increases.

*March* — Agreement was reached between the federal government and Interprovincial Pipe Line Limited covering the construction of a crude oil pipeline extension from Sarnia to Montreal.

*April* — A First Ministers' Conference on Energy was held on April 9-10 but no consensus was reached as to the timing and amount of the next crude oil price increase.

— The Petroleum Administration Act was passed by the House of Commons on April 30 and subsequent by the Senate and received Royal Assent in May.

*May* — The Minister of Energy, Mines and Resources announced further changes with respect to the pricing of natural gas exports to the United States. Prices were to rise to $1.40/Mcf effective August 1, 1975 and to $1.60 effective November 1.

*June* — The Federal Budget provided for the increase in the crude oil price to $8.00/barrel, from $6.50; a special 10 cent excise tax on motor gasoline for non-commercial use; the increase to $1.25/Mcf effective November 1, 1975, of the Toronto city-gate price of Alberta natural gas; and an increased tax incentive to those companies that increased exploration activities.

— Canada/United States understanding was reached on oil "swapping" arrangements.

*July* — Federal government oil price guidelines were announced to provide for an increase in the wholesale price of oil products, equivalent to the $1.50/barrel increase in crude oil, effective 45 days following July 1 when the crude oil price increase became effective.

— The Minister of Energy, Mines and Resources commented on the recently issued National Energy Board report on natural gas demand, supply and deliverability which drew attention to the fact that natural gas supplies would not be adequate in the near term to meet both projected increases in domestic demand and existing export commitments.

— The Oil Import Compensation Program was amended so that compensation for crude oil imports would be paid on a flat rate basis rather than using rates varying with crude type, source and landing points.

— Legislation to establish a National Petroleum Company, Petro-Canada, was approved by Parliament.

— The Minister of Energy, Mines and Resources announced that the federal government had approved participation by Petro-Canada in the Polar Gas Study Group.

*August*      — The National Energy Board announced that hearings on the Mackenzie Valley Pipeline applications would commence on October 27.

*September*    — The National Energy Board issued its second oil export report.

— An agreement on natural gas pricing and on the flowback to producers of extra revenue from gas at the higher export price was reached between the federal and Alberta governments.

*November*    — The natural gas city-gate price of $1.25 per Mcf in the eastern zone, as announced in the June budget, took effect on November 1.

*December*     — Canada, as co-chairman, played an important part in the launching of the Conference on International Economic Cooperation (CIEC) and is participating directly in the work of the two commissions dealing with energy and de- development.

— An Energy Ministers' Conference was held on December 12 on energy supply and demand, conservation, pricing and energy research and development.

**1976**

*January*
— Petro-Canada began operations on January 1.
— Negotiations were concluded by Canada and United States officials on the text of a Pipeline Agreement which was then referred to the respective governments for review and approval with a view, in due course, to signature and ratification.

*February*
— Minister of Energy, Mines and Resources announced a number of new energy conservation programs including mileage standards for automobiles sold in Canada, energy-efficiency guidelines for buildings, minimum energy standards for appliances, support of energy conservation through existing industrial assistance programs and lower energy consumption by federal departments and agencies.

*March*
— An Energy Ministers' Conference was held on March 5 to discuss oil and gas pricing, treatment of oil inventories, oil industry financing, energy conservation, northern pipelines, and the International Energy Agency.
— Minister of Energy, Mines and Resources announced new funding for energy research and development.
— The federal government announced that, as an interim measure pending the National Energy Board's hearing and decision on Interprovincial Pipe Line Limited's system tolls, it would meet the cost of shipping western Canadian oil from Toronto to Montreal.

*April*
— The National Energy Board started hearings

on competing proposals for overland movement of Alaskan and Mackenzie Delta gas.

*May*            — A federal-provincial agreement to raise domestic natural gas prices to 85% of BTU equiva-
lent oil price was reached.

*June*           — The Interprovincial Pipeline began continuous
delivery of crude from Sarnia to Montreal.
                 — The National Energy Board approved con-
struction of 765 kv transmission line for export of surplus power by Hydro Quebec to
United States.

*August*         — Canadian crude oil exchange with the United
States to facilitate supply of feedstocks to
Northern Tier refineries was approved.

*October*        — The National Energy Board accepted the proposal of Foothills Pipeline (Yukon) in hear-
ings on transportation of northern gas.

*November*       — The Syncrude tar sands project was reorgan-
ized to include participation of federal and
provincial governments.
                 — The National Energy Board announced separ-
ate determination of light and heavy crude oil
export volumes.

*December*       — An application was filed by Kitimat Pipeline
to build crude oil line for moving Alaskan oil
across Canada to Northern U.S. refineries.

**1977**

*January*        — Canadian-U.S. pipeline agreement providing
for transit guaranties was signed.

*February*       — A Federal Power Commission Administrative
Law Judge decision recommended approval of
Alaskan Arctic Gas Pipeline proposal.
                 — The first data on West Pembina oil discovery
indicating major new field was released.
                 — The National Energy Board approved short-
term emergency gas exports.

                  — Federal Power Commission approved seasonal exchanges of Canadian gas for U.S. electricity.

*March*             — An amended Alcan pipeline application was filed with the Federal Power Commission and the National Energy Board.

*April*               — British Columbia allowed Pan Alberta Pipeline to export additional gas to West Coast Transmission.

*May*                 — The Federal Power Commission recommended overland pipelines as superior to the El Paso proposal.

                  — Berger Commission report recommended against proceeding with Arctic Gas project at this time on environmental and socio-economic grounds.

                  — Canada raised the gas export price to Can $2.25 (U.S. $2.16)/Mcf.

*June*              — Kitimat Pipeline requested suspension of its pipeline proposal and supported application of Trans Mountain Pipeline.

*July*               — A request was filed with the National Energy Board for permission to test in situ tar sand extraction in Peace River region.

                  — The Canadian government promulgated interim leasing regulations for crown lands providing for increased exploration incentives. Federal and provincial governments agreed on sharing of oil and gas revenues, staged oil and gas price increases.

                  — The Canadian government ended its freeze on frontier exploration permits.

                  — A National Energy Board decision approved proposal of Foothills (Yukon) Pipeline (Canadian section of Alcan), with modifications.

*August*          — The Canadian Government endorsed the Alcan pipeline proposal.

                  — The U.S. Senate ratified pipeline transit agreement.

*September* — President Carter selected Alcan pipeline over other pending applications.

— The U.S. and Canadian governments signed pipeline transit agreement.

— The National Energy Board approved application of Manitoba Hydro for construction of a 500 kv power line to the international border.

*October* — The Federal Power Commission approved importation of Canadian gas at an increased price (U.S. $2.16/Mcf).

*November* — Congress approved the Alcan pipeline route for Alaskan gas.

— The Imperial Oil Company slated construction of a plant for extracting oil from Alberta sands, subject to government support.

— Trans Mountain Pipeline withdrew its proposal for moving Alaskan crude inland after Congress prohibited expansion of port facilities.

— U.S. and Canadian officials discussed terms of a comprehensive trade package, including several energy projects.

*December* — Polar Gas Pipeline filed application for shipment of gas from Arctic Islands to Ontario.

— The Canadian government agreed to exchange Canadian for foreign crude.

— The National Energy Board approved proposal by Tenneco group to construct terminal and regasification plant in New Brunswick for supply of U.S. and Canadian markets.

**1978**

*January* — The U.S. and Canadian governments signed an agreement to encourage closer cooperation on a wide range of energy projects.

— Large gas discoveries in Alberta and British Columbia were reported.

*February*  — The Kitimat Pipeline proposal was rejected by the Canadian government on environmental grounds.

*April*  — The Canadian House of Commons approved construction of the Canadian segment of the Alcan pipeline.

Sources: Pre-1973: Ministry of Energy, Mines and Resources, *An Energy Policy for Canada, Phase 1,* Volume II (1973), p. 307; 1973–March 1976: Ministry of Energy, Mines and Resources, *An Energy Strategy for Canada* (1976), pp. 152-155; April 1976–: compiled by the authors from various official and press sources.

# Appendix F

## Canada's Future Energy
## Investment Requirements

**Figure F-1. Canadian Components of Energy Investment, 1976-1990 (high-price scenario)**

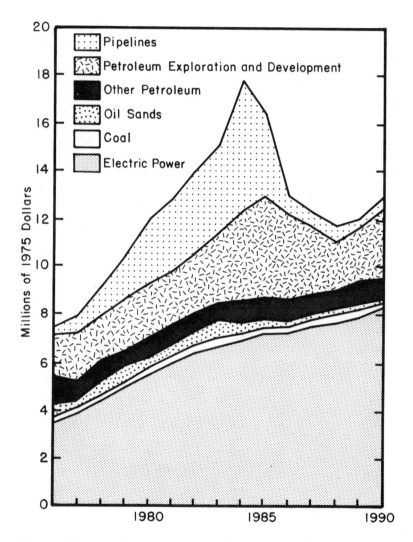

Source: Ministry of Energy, Mines and Resources, *An Energy Strategy for Canada,* 1976, p. 107.

**Table F-1. Estimated Canadian Energy-Related Capital Requirements, 1976-1990**

|  | *(High-Price Scenario, billions of 1975 dollars)* | | | |
| --- | --- | --- | --- | --- |
|  | *1976-80* | *1981-85* | *1986-90* | *Total* |
| Electric power | 21.7 | 32.5 | 37.0 | 91.2 |
| Pipelines | 5.7 | 19.2 | 3.0 | 27.9 |
| Petroleum |  |  |  |  |
|   Exploration and development | 10.6 | 15.5 | 14.2 | 40.3 |
|   Refining and marketing | 3.9 | 4.1 | 4.8 | 12.8 |
|   Oil sands | 3.0 | 2.3 | .3 | 5.6 |
| Coal[a] | .8 | 1.5 | .9 | 3.2 |
| Energy investment | 45.7 | 75.1 | 60.2 | 181.0 |
| Estimated GNP | 912.1 | 1,162.0 | 1,438.5 | 3,512.6 |
| Energy investment as % of GNP | 5.0 | 6.5 | 4.2 | 5.2 |

[a] The estimates related to coal do not include estimates of new investment necessary to upgrade transportation systems.

Source: Ministry of Energy, Mines and Resources, *An Energy Strategy for Canada,* 1976, p. 108.